Parents often ask me for informat. ...at can help them communicate with young people about alcohol and drug use. At last here is a book that is engagingly written yet provides a wealth of relevant advice, information, and case studies. With this book Glenn Williams builds on his reputation for providing balanced and intelligent advice.

John Toumbourou
Professor and Chair in Health Psychology,
Deakin University

Nobody has done more to help parents all across the world deal with the issue of drugs and their children. I highly commend this book to you.

Rob Parsons
Executive Chairman, Care for the Family
Author, *Bringing Home the Prodigals*

TALKING
SMACK

TALKING SMACK

WHO'S SPEAKING TO YOUR KIDS ABOUT DRUGS AND ALCOHOL, IF YOU'RE NOT?

GLENN WILLIAMS

Authentic

To my children, Ben, Ryan, and Chloe

Authentic Publishing
A Ministry of Biblica
We welcome your questions and comments.

USA	1820 Jet Stream Drive, Colorado Springs, CO 80921
	www.authenticbooks.com
India	Logos Bhavan, Medchal Road, Jeedimetla Village, Secunderabad
	500 055, A.P.

Talking Smack
ISBN-13: 978-1-93406-886-1

12 11 10 / 6 5 4 3 2 1
Published in 2010 by Authentic

A catalog record for this book is available through the Library of Congress.

Printed in the United States of America

Names and details in some of the true stories contained herein have been changed
to protect the privacy of individuals involved.

Contents

Foreword   xi

Introduction   1

Part 1: Questions All Parents Need to Ask

Chapter 1: Getting Involved   13
> Why is it important for me to talk to my children about drugs and alcohol?

Chapter 2: The Allure   27
> Why do children use drugs and alcohol?

Chapter 3: The Basics   45
> How do I get started in talking with my children about drugs and alcohol?

Chapter 4: For Parents of Younger Children   63
> How do I protect my preschooler or elementary-age child from drugs and alcohol?

Chapter 5: A Safe Place   79
> How do I set healthy boundaries for my children?

Chapter 6: For Parents of Older Children   91
> How do I protect my middle schooler or high schooler from drugs and alcohol?

Chapter 7: Intervention 103

    What can I do if I suspect (or know) that my teen is
already drinking or using drugs?

Part 2: Interview with a Mother and Daughter

Chapter 8: Reality Preparation 121

    "We truly want to help protect you."

Chapter 9: The Learning Incident 137

    "I think I'm going to die!"

Chapter 10: Facing the Consequences 153

    "What are we going to do with this?"

Conclusion 163

Appendix: Resources 167

Notes 171

FOREWORD

G lenn Williams recently told me a story that illustrates precisely why this book is so important. He was in Australia promoting How to Drug Proof Your Kids, a curriculum he developed to help parents steer their children away from the dangers of drug and alcohol abuse. One pastor told Glenn that How to Drug Proof Your Kids simply wasn't a necessary resource for his congregation. After all, his church was located in an affluent suburb and most of the kids came from relatively healthy, stable homes.

A few weeks later, that same pastor called Glenn in desperation. As it turned out, his own child, as well as several other kids from the church youth group, were actively experimenting with marijuana. The illusion that his congregation—and indeed, his own family—was "safe" from the influence of illegal drugs had been shattered.

I can't state it any more plainly than this: If you're a parent, you *need* to read this book. Drug and alcohol abuse do not discriminate. They impact children in every nation and every environment and every walk of life. No matter how compliant or well behaved your children are, please don't put your head in the sand and think that you won't have to confront this issue with them at some point. Drugs pollute both the ghetto and the country club. They are found in both public and private schools. They can be found in urban and rural environments, and everywhere in between.

Regardless of cultural background or socioeconomic status, no one ever grew up *wanting* to be an addict. But somewhere along the way, he or she believed the lie that the abuse of drugs or binge drinking was nothing more than harmless fun or a way to blunt emotional pain. And by that point, it was too late to turn back. Drugs and alcohol have a way of deluding users into believing that they can somehow remain in control, even as they engage in an activity that destroys both body and soul.

As president of Focus on the Family, I see evidence of this all too often. Every day the staff at Focus receive e-mails, phone calls, and letters from individuals and families teetering on the brink of collapse as a result of drugs and alcohol. What began as "innocent experimentation" quickly descended into a nightmare of addiction. It's incredibly difficult to learn about a teenager caught up in a pattern of drug or alcohol abuse, but it's equally traumatic to read of the pain and sorrow endured by his parents. In most cases, they are caught completely off guard by the revelation of their child's addiction. They didn't think it could happen in their family. By the time they are made aware of the problem, their precious child has been arrested or has overdosed . . . or worse.

This is a bleak picture. But take heart! There are a number of steps that you, as a parent, can take to avoid scenarios like those I have just described. And that's what *Talking Smack: Who's Speaking with Your Kids about Drugs and Alcohol, If You're Not?* is all about. Glenn has spent years in the trenches developing and teaching the How to Drug Proof Your Kids curriculum, and the wisdom and experience he has gained through that process are reflected in the book you're now holding. Within these pages you'll find solid advice on how to talk to your kids honestly and openly about drugs and how to steer them toward making healthy decisions when temptation and peer pressure come knocking.

But perhaps you feel like you've already failed. Maybe your kids are well into their teen years and, if not using drugs or alcohol themselves, have formed wrong opinions about these substances—based on negative input from their peers and youth culture—that are troubling. Rest assured that there is advice for *you* in this book too. It's not too late to intervene and to guide your child in a more positive direction. As you become intentional in modeling healthy behavior that aligns with the parental advice you're sharing, you'll be sending consistent messages that will impact your children as they wrestle with their own decisions over drugs and alcohol.

We all make mistakes as parents, and just as we extend grace to our children when they veer from the straight and narrow, so will our kids extend grace to us when we're transparent and honest about our mistakes. And even if you've missed opportunities to talk to your kids about drugs in the past—or if you're worried that your attempts to broach the subject have fallen on deaf ears—this book will encourage you not to give up.

In many ways, talking to kids about drugs and alcohol can be even scarier for parents than talking to them about sex. Sometimes we'd rather just gloss over a subject than bring it out in the open. We might fear introducing mature subject matter such as sex and drugs too early. Or perhaps we're afraid our kids will ask us questions that we can't answer. The beauty of this book is that it will leave you, as a parent, feeling empowered, confident, and informed when it comes to talking to your kids about drugs and alcohol. Will the conversation be uncomfortable? Possibly. But just remember that this is a topic that *will* confront your children at some point, if it hasn't already. It's so much better to get the issue out on the table now and to talk honestly and openly with them, rather than to wait for their peers, or their favorite music or movie stars, to "educate" them.

I have a vested interest in this subject because my wife, Jean, and I have two boys at home who, as of this writing, are ages nine and seven. We desperately want to help them do the right thing when it comes to the issue of drugs and alcohol. I have known Glenn Williams for more than sixteen years, and we have talked at length about our desire to apply the How to Drug Proof Your Kids principles to our own homes and families. That's why I'm so thankful for this book.

There are no guarantees, of course. Sometimes parents who make every effort to instill positive virtues and values in their kids must endure the pain of seeing them reject those principles later on. As I have already noted, Glenn has provided some practical insights and resources for those who find themselves in this heart-wrenching position. At some point, we all have to realize that we don't have complete control over the choices our kids make. Nevertheless, this book will go a long way toward giving you the confidence and information you need to help steer your kids in the right direction.

Talking Smack is a timely resource for every parent. I'm grateful to Glenn Williams for his friendship and for his willingness to share this important work with me as well as with mothers and fathers all over the world who long to see their children avoid the seductive trap of drug and alcohol abuse.

Jim Daly
President and CEO, Focus on the Family

INTRODUCTION

After a night at the movies, Jackie and Bryan Wyman and their thirteen-year-old daughter, Lisa, pulled into the driveway of their home. They were about to experience something that would later replay in their minds over and over.

The couple first sensed something was wrong when they saw all the lights blazing in the house and the front door standing open. Then they noticed their son, fifteen-year-old Gary, sitting on the front lawn, crying.

Bryan braked the car to a screeching halt, and he and Jackie ran to their son. Now they could see that Gary was covered with cuts and bruises.

"Gary, what happened? What's wrong?"

Still crying and upset, Gary was unable to piece together a sentence that made any sense. So Jackie lifted Gary to his feet and helped him walk toward the house. Bryan, meanwhile, rushed ahead to check out the house.

When Jackie and Gary walked in, trailed by Lisa, Bryan was looking around the living room and shaking his head in disbelief. The place was a mess and some of the family's valuables were missing. Noticeably absent were the large-screen television, the DVD player, and the stereo system, their empty places marked by the smashed remains of glass and walnut panels from the electronics case.

Bryan and Jackie turned again to their son. "Gary?"

Slowly the story unfolded.

Between sobs, Gary broke the news that he had been smoking marijuana three or four times a week over the last few months. When he lost his after-school job, he couldn't afford the drugs anymore. The supplier extended him a line of credit, but Gary wasn't able to meet the terms. On this night, his supplier had come to collect in another way—and to teach Gary a lesson.

Of course Jackie and Bryan comforted their son and saw to his immediate needs. But at the same time there began in their hearts a process of dealing with the news they'd been handed. They'd had no idea that Gary was using drugs. What were they to make of it?

Jackie was heartbroken, and her reaction was primarily to criticize herself. Questions like these assailed her:

Where did I go wrong as a mother? How could I not have seen the signs?

Why didn't Gary talk to me sooner? Was I that unapproachable? Did he think I would stop loving him?

Did Lisa know about Gary's drug use? Why wouldn't she tell me if she knew something? How do I handle this with Lisa to make sure she doesn't go down the same path as her brother?

Bryan dealt with the situation differently. He refused to believe that his son had a problem with drugs. To him, it seemed that Gary was going through a phase typical for teenagers.

Bryan's thought process went something like this:

Smoking marijuana isn't such a big deal. I smoked a few joints during my college years, after all.

Sure, Gary got into some trouble, but hopefully this will be the end of it. At least he doesn't owe anybody any money, since his supplier has recovered what he was owed.

Maybe it would be better if we all forgot about this situation as quickly as possible and went on with our lives. Giving too much attention to Gary's drug use might even make things worse.

In reality, Bryan's denial of the problem was no more productive than was his wife's blaming of herself. Drugs had entered the Wyman household, and the parents needed to do something effective in dealing with it. In fact, they should have been preparing for this possibility for years.

Hope for Your Family

Lots of families are like the Wymans before the night of the robbery. The parents think that if they have a normal, healthy family life, their children won't do drugs or drink alcohol as minors. That only happens in dysfunctional families, they think. It only happens to *bad* kids. "That's not how we raised our children," many parents would smugly say.

Or so they would say until they come home from the movies and find their house robbed and their child beat up.

Or until they are asked to come to the school to meet with the principal to talk about a "situation."

Or until they are searching for something in their child's bedroom and come upon bottles of hard liquor in the closet.

Or until they get a call from the police station saying their child has been booked for drug possession.

Reality has a way of stomping all over our stereotypical views.

I'm going to assume, though, that since you have picked up *Talking Smack*, you are not the complacent sort of parent. You recognize that drugs and alcohol really can worm their way into the family you love. (Or maybe that's already happened.) You take the threat seriously and want to do something about it.

Good for you. There's hope for your family. By dealing with the dangers of drug and alcohol abuse head-on and communicating well with your children, you can significantly reduce the risk that substance abuse poses to your family.

> By dealing with the dangers of drug and alcohol abuse head-on and communicating well with your children, you can significantly reduce the risk that substance abuse poses to your family.

The idea behind this book—proven to be true time and again—is that *the best way for parents to protect their kids from the threats posed by drugs and alcohol is to maintain loving, informed two-way communication with them throughout their growing-up years.* This book will teach you what you need to know about discussing drugs and alcohol with your kids from their early years right on up to the time when they are ready to take their place in the adult world. (And by the way, the parenting principles addressed in this book are relevant for other challenges you will face as you help your children make good decisions in many areas of life.)

Thousands of parents just like you have taken the advice contained in the book and have used it to safeguard their children. Those parents are so glad they did. I know—I hear it from them all the time! You'll be glad too.

The Wymans did too little too late to protect their kids. You don't need to make the same mistake.

Where the Information Comes From

The information in this book comes from two important and reliable sources.

• *Substance abuse education.* First, in this book I draw on more than twenty years of experience in working professionally with parents and children in the area of substance abuse. Some of this experience has come through counseling individual families, and some of it has come through providing drug education to larger groups.

In 1999, as the CEO of Focus on the Family Australia, I launched a program called How to Drug Proof Your Kids. (See *www.drugproofyourkids.com* for more information.) The response was overwhelming. Today this program is operating in more than a dozen countries in Asia, North America, Europe, Africa, and the Middle East. Sixty thousand parents have attended the program so far, and the number is steadily growing.

If you have already attended a How to Drug Proof Your Kids workshop, this book will serve as reinforcement of what you learned and as a much more detailed conversation guide to use with your children than you received in the program.

If you have not participated in the program—no worries. This book stands on its own as a guide for speaking with your kids. And you can be confident in it because it is the fruit of my experience with literally thousands of families much like your own.

• *My own parenting.* Second, and equally as important, I write as a father of three children who are just as much at risk from drugs and alcohol as are any other children. My wife, Natalie, and I are the parents of Ben, Ryan, and Chloe. We love these kids dearly, and we want to do whatever we can to keep anything bad from happening to them. That's why we have implemented the principles in this book with our own kids.

> You can be confident in *Talking Smack* because it is the fruit of my experience with literally thousands of families much like your own.

Because I'm a father, I know how important this topic is. And because I'm a father, I know that the subject of substance abuse is emotionally loaded and not always easy to bring up with kids. So, if you sense realism and passion in this book (and I believe you will), it is because this is such a personal subject for me.

Throughout the book, I will occasionally bring in stories of my own experiences in trying to protect my three kids from drugs. I think that you will find that you can relate to these stories as you get a glimpse of one dad trying to take care of his kids.

The *Talking Smack* Promises

I know that the information in *Talking Smack* works. That's why I'm so eager to share it with you. So as we begin, let me make some promises to you:

- *Talking Smack* **is values based.** You'll find none of the children-need-to-make-up-their-own-minds-about-drug-use-and-underage-drinking attitude in this book. I believe that parents are parents and children are children. Parents need to protect their kids from the harm of drug and alcohol abuse by giving them important skills and reliable information that will help them to make wise choices even in the face of significant pressure.

- *Talking Smack* **is for both younger and older children.** Many experts, when addressing parents about drug and alcohol abuse, focus on teenagers only. That's a mistake. Although the problems most often surface in the teenage years, younger children need to start learning lessons about drugs and alcohol in a way they can understand. *Talking Smack* helps you to know how to teach those lessons in an age-appropriate way for kids as young as preschoolers.

- *Talking Smack* **is realistic.** I'm not going to assume that your family looks like it is ready to head out to Sunday school at any moment, that your children are always obedient, or that your own past is spotless. I know you live in the real world, a place where you are struggling to be the best parent you can be and where your kids face real threats from drugs and alcohol. So you'll get honesty and truth in the pages of this book.

- *Talking Smack* **is practical.** Although everything in this book is consistent with sound research in the subject, the book does not dwell on theories. It is based primarily on experience, namely my own experiences as a parent and the experiences of the thousands of parents I have helped in this area. So you know that it makes sense and that it works—and will work for you.

- *Talking Smack* **is easy to use.** You're a busy person. Obviously—you're a parent! Boy, don't I know how it is. And that's why I have kept this book short and filled it with a combination of inspirational stories and easily picked up pointers. You'll find the book a quick read that you can get around in easily and can turn back to whenever you need a refresher on the subject. You might even find it kind of fun.

What it comes down to is this:

You don't have to just pray that substance abuse will never make inroads into your family.

You don't have to just hope that your kids are learning what they need to know about drugs and alcohol through school, church, or other youth programs.

You don't have to keep putting off talking about drugs and alcohol with your kids because you don't know what to say.

With *Talking Smack*, you will learn how to have conversations with your kids that will help them make it into adulthood free of the harm that comes from drugs and alcohol. We'll start with the questions that are most on parents' minds about this subject—and the answers that can get you started on effective communication with your kids.

PART 1

Questions All Parents Need to Ask

GETTING INVOLVED

Why is it important for me to talk to my children about drugs and alcohol?

D espite their popular association with having a good time, drug abuse and underage drinking threaten our children with many kinds of harm. These are some of them:

- unhealthy friendships that can sometimes become destructive
- dysfunctional behavior in the family
- declining performance at school
- increased risk of disease and poor health
- low self-esteem and confidence
- poor decision-making skills
- financial drain
- date rape
- addiction
- criminal arrest
- death

As parents, you and I don't want our children to have to deal with any of these problems. We want to help our kids if they get involved with drugs and alcohol. And even better, if possible, we would like to help them avoid such behaviors in the first place.

That's what this book is all about. It teaches parents how to establish loving, informed communication about substance abuse with their children that can continue throughout the growing-up years. Talking with our kids regularly and well is the key to keeping them safe from drugs and alcohol.

> Talking with our kids regularly and well is the key to keeping them safe from drugs and alcohol.

It sounds simple and in a way it is. But as a drug educator and counselor, I know that parents have lots of questions when the subject comes up. We're going to be dealing with the most-asked questions one by one in the first part of this book. I know that these are the most-asked questions because they are based on more than fifteen thousand surveys turned in by participants in my How to Drug Proof Your Kids program.

The first question is this: "Why is it important for me to talk to my child about drugs and alcohol?"

At first blush that might sound like a silly question. After all, we know about the risks presented by drugs and alcohol— the damage to health, the possibility of addiction, and all the rest. Substance abuse is bad for a person. *That's* why it's important to talk to our kids about these issues!

Yet I have discovered that many parents really are asking this question, if not openly, then implicitly. The truth is, they'd rather not bring up a sensitive topic like this with their kids, and so they just don't . . . until a crisis occurs in their family that forces them to deal with the issue.

How tragic that in many cases those crises—with all the pain that comes with them—could have been prevented if the parents had been proactive in discussing drinking and drugs with their kids. Parents with even a little hesitation about opening up this topic with their children need help getting past whatever is holding them back.

Parents' Common Fears

When a parent asks me, "Why should I talk to my kids about drugs and alcohol?" I know there must be some kind of fear underlying the skepticism. Something is motivating the parent to look for an excuse to avoid taking responsibility in this area. I find it's best to sift through the parent's feelings, identify the fear, and bring it up to examine it.

Parents may have any number of fears in this area, but three come up most often. As we consider each one, remember this: while these fears may be legitimate in their own way, none of them is an adequate excuse for choosing not to talk with your child about drugs. The simple fact is, *your fears about discussing drugs and alcohol are not as important as the threat those substances represent.*

See if you find any of these fears lurking in your own heart:

Fear of creating the problem. Some parents believe that, if they bring up the issue of substance abuse, their children may be tempted to experiment with drugs or alcohol. *Rather than* *arouse my children's curiosity about destructive behaviors,* they wonder, *wouldn't I be better off ignoring the subject?*

The answer is no. As we'll be seeing later in this chapter, kids are already much more exposed to drugs and alcohol than most parents realize. By talking to them about the subject, we won't be giving them ideas; we'll be helping them to see the risks.

Fear of coming across as ignorant. Many parents are aware that they don't know much about drug and alcohol abuse, and so they are worried about losing credibility in the eyes of their children if they starting talking about the subject. And for some, this is a genuine possibility.

But rather than not saying anything about substance abuse, it's better to educate ourselves so that we can talk knowledgeably on the subject. That's what this book enables its readers to do.

Fear of having to fess up. Some parents worry that if they raise the subject of substance abuse with their children then their children may ask personal questions about their own history. "Mom, did you ever experiment with drugs? Dad, did you ever go binge-drinking with your friends?" The answer might be yes. And then what? Will the children take the parents' own experience as a license to experiment with controlled substances?

Like the first two, this is an understandable fear. But as we'll be discovering later in the book, you have choices about what you will reveal and how you will reveal it. There are options for discussing your own experiences that can make your anti-drug message *more* effective with your children, not *less* effective.

Well, I know that your fears may not be entirely laid to rest at this point. That's okay. We'll be learning much more about how to overcome your fears in later chapters. In the meantime, let me share some possibly surprising and undoubtedly scary facts with you that should help you overcome any resistance you may have to the idea of talking about drugs and alcohol with your kids.

No Information Vacuum

Let's be realistic: Your kids aren't going to go through life never hearing about drinking and drug taking. They will get messages about these behaviors from some source or other.

One of the main sources is the daily bombardment of images and messages from the media. Tuning in to the top forty on the radio, going to see the latest movie blockbuster, or reading about how celebrities ended up in rehab makes it almost impossible for your child not to be exposed to drugs.

And even if you could block all media from your kids (good luck with that!), they would still hear drugs and alcohol being discussed among their friends. At school, at parties, or in friends' homes, your children can hardly avoid either hearing about these substances or witnessing their use.

So here's a basic fact: *If you don't talk to your children about drugs and alcohol, someone else will.* And will that person give your children accurate information? Does he share your beliefs and values? Will she discourage your children from using drugs and alcohol, or will she perhaps encourage them to "harmlessly" experiment?

I don't want my children to learn about drugs from someone who doesn't have to take responsibility for the consequences.

As a parent of three children, I don't want my children to learn about drugs from someone who doesn't have to take responsibility for the consequences. Neither do you, I'm sure. And neither did a man named Tim.

I met Tim in the lounge of an auto shop where I was having my muffler replaced. We struck up a conversation and eventually got around to what I do for a job, including training parents in how to talk with their children about drugs. With a look of amazement on his face, Tim blurted out that he had recently completed the program I started: How to Drug Proof Your Kids.

"Really?" I said, as amazed as he was.

"Yes. I found it so empowering," he said.

"I'm glad to hear that. But tell me something. You said your oldest child is only in kindergarten. So why did you participate in the program so early?"

That's when Tim explained that his motivation for attending the program related to his experience as a teenager.

When Tim was in high school, he desperately wanted to belong to a "cool" group of students. That meant he soon found himself hanging out with some friends who were doing things they shouldn't have been doing. It all started relatively innocently with smoking cigarettes. Then one of Tim's friends got his hands on some marijuana, and they shared it around. They knew that it was wrong and that their parents would flip if they found out, but they didn't think it was too bad.

Things began getting out of control over the next few months. The teens used marijuana more and more frequently. As a result, they started missing school. They fell behind in their homework, and their grades began falling.

Tim said, "I'm sure my parents must have noticed something, but they never said anything. That was part of the problem. Not once did they ever speak to me about drugs—not even when I came home stoned!"

He continued, "My life was messed up for a number of years after I finished school. When I became a parent, I said to myself, 'There's no way I want my kids to be messed up by doing the same stupid things.'"

He came home from work one evening and began flipping through the local newspaper. There it was—an advertisement placed by his son's kindergarten encouraging parents to attend the How to Drug Proof Your Kids program.

"I couldn't help but think how cool that was," said Tim. "I mean, educating parents while their children are still young, before drugs become an issue. My wife and I arranged a babysitter for our two young children, and we went to the program. How I wish that my parents knew what I know now! I'm sure it would have made a difference for me when I was a kid. I know it will make a difference for my kids."

Tim's parents didn't talk to him about drugs, but someone else did—the very friends who introduced him to drug use. Fortunately, Tim managed to turn his life around from the negative impact of drugs. And influenced by his own experience, he made sure that he and his wife were taking the initiative in talking to their own children, rather than leaving this responsibility to someone else.

Someone else will teach our kids about drugs and alcohol if we don't—that's the first truth to remember. But there's more.

A Drug- and Booze-filled Culture

A few years ago, when I was living in Melbourne, Australia, I happened to read a news report revealing that drug traffickers were going to schools and handing out heroin starter kits to children as young as ten. I couldn't believe it. I actually reread the article to see if I had misread it the first time. But it was true.

I was shocked. The notion that children were being pressured to try a dangerous drug at such a young age disturbed me greatly. These kids didn't have the maturity or understanding to realize how their choices would affect their lives.

Of course, I realized that not all ten-year-old children are confronted with this scenario. Still, that news report served as a wake-up call for me. What I came to understand, and what all parents must understand, is this: *drugs and alcohol are part of our culture—our kids* will *be impacted by them.* There is no avoiding them.

From your experience, you might be thinking this is an exaggeration. "Drugs are not readily available in my child's school or neighborhood," you might say. "There's some drinking among the older kids, sure, but our community is adequately policed, and the incidents of substance abuse are really quite rare."

My friend, I wish that were the case. Alcohol and drug abuse are much more widespread than most of us realize.

They come in many forms and happen all the time, including among the young.

Surprisingly to many, a big proportion of the drug abuse that goes on involves the misuse of prescription drugs. As dependence on legal drugs by adults continues to escalate, these drugs become more available for kids to pick up and experiment with. Drugs used to regulate blood pressure, reduce anxiety, facilitate sleep, eliminate migraine headaches, remove the pain from an injury, treat depression, and stay alert are all favorites of kids wanting to try drugs.

Meanwhile, binge drinking has almost become an epidemic in our society among teenagers and college students. Rave parties have become synonymous with ecstasy and other designer drugs. And more often than not, sporting victories celebrated by our children have become a form of secular baptism where teammates are immersed in alcohol, reminiscent of an ancient Roman orgy.

Okay, I got a little carried away with the last sentence, but the truth is still inescapable. Drugs and alcohol are normal parts of our society and therefore of our children's lives. Knowing what to say and how to respond is critical if we want to give our children a positive future—and possibly even save their lives.

And that's still not all. I've saved the most important truth for last.

More Than Just a "Good" Parent

If there is one message that all parents must hear on this subject, it is that their children are not immune to the pressure to drink and use drugs. We might be good parents, and our kids might be good kids, but they are still at risk.

I have been with a number of parents who have lost their children to drugs. It's tragic every time. Few things break my heart more. But every time, the educator in me wants to learn from the situation, so I start asking questions.

Had they talked to their child about drugs? Some of them had, but not all of them. Why not? They wanted to believe that their child would never get involved in drugs. After all, their child was raised in a happy, healthy home. She had good friends who would often be invited home after school or on the weekend. Each Sunday the family would go to church.

And still the child is dead. Why?

As parents, we naturally want to believe the best about our children. This attitude is a blessing. It helps us to love our children unconditionally and to do all we can to give them a bright future. But the attitude is also a curse. It can lull us into a false sense of security in which we are unable to see the challenges facing our children and therefore don't impart to them the wisdom and strategies they need.

We believe that by instilling in our children values and attitudes important to us, we will discourage them from experimenting with drugs. The truth is that, while sometimes this is enough, too often it is not.

Research does provide some encouragement to parents. It shows that by being a model to our children, talking to them about illicit substances, and educating them about the consequences of using these substances, the likelihood that they will experiment with drugs and alcohol is dramatically reduced.[1] The disturbing fact that lingers, however, is that *even if you're a great parent, your child still might use drugs or alcohol.*

Karen was a great parent who thought her two daughters would never do drugs. She shared a wonderful relationship with her husband and children and even once or twice discussed drugs with the girls. Her children were doing well at school, had great friends, and seemed amazingly happy.

By being a model to our children, talking to them about illicit substances, and educating them about the consequences of using these substances, the likelihood that they will experiment with drugs and alcohol is dramatically reduced.

Then one night Karen's world fell apart.

"My husband and I had just gone to bed when the telephone rang," Karen explained to me. "It wasn't unusual for the phone to ring after ten p.m., as we had told our girls to call us anytime if they needed to be picked up from their friends' houses or wherever they might be. But this time I was confused when I picked up the receiver, because I couldn't make sense of the hysterical voice on the other end."

Eventually Karen realized it was her eighteen-year-old daughter, Sandy, on the line. Sandy was trying to explain that her fifteen-year-old sister, Melinda, had collapsed at the party they had attended and that the paramedics were having trouble reviving her.

Karen and her husband, Mark, sped to the hospital, where they found Sandy sobbing uncontrollably. Melinda had been pronounced dead. They learned later that Melinda had taken an ecstasy tablet—just one—and had become dehydrated.

According to her sister, this was Melinda's first experience with drugs.

"Words cannot capture how I felt at this point," Karen recalled. "It is an experience I wish upon no parent. For months, I constantly felt as though I were drowning, as though my lungs were about to burst as I struggled to the surface to gasp for air."

Sapped of all energy, and seemingly of life itself, she began the grueling task of a parent's postmortem. *Where did I go wrong? Why didn't I see this coming? What could I have done differently? Was I too trusting? She was such a great girl; did I fail her as a parent?* At times Karen became crushed by the burden of guilt.

"I learned that drugs do not discriminate on the basis of family, age, gender, or level of education," she said. "For me, they took away a beautiful gift I only got to enjoy for such a short time."

After losing Melinda, Karen met with many parents and their children who were dealing with drugs. She learned things about preventing drug use that she wishes she had known earlier. If she had known those things, it may not have guaranteed the life of her daughter. But on the other hand, it might have made all the difference.

We'll look at the kinds of things that Karen learned in the chapters ahead. These will help you be not just a *good* parent but also a *prepared* parent. One who knows how to have regular, natural, positive discussions about drugs and alcohol with your children so that you can conduct them safely through their childhood years. The next step is learning why children want to use drugs and alcohol.

Parenting for Drug-Free Kids: A Quiz

1. How often, if at all, have you spoken to your children about drugs and alcohol? _____

2. What fears are holding you back from talking more often, or more effectively, about these topics with your children? _____

3. Thinking about the people in your children's sphere of acquaintances, who might try to tempt them to take drugs or drink alcohol? _____

4. Where might your children have access to drugs and alcohol? _____

5. In what way might you be overconfident about your relationship with your child—to the point that it could be blinding you to the risk your child is facing?

_____

6. When was the last time you looked in your medicine cabinet to make sure "old" prescriptions had been properly discarded? _____

Chapter 1 Summary

Reasons you should talk to your children about drugs and alcohol:

- Your fears about discussing drugs and alcohol are not as important as the threat those substances represent.
- If you don't talk to your kids about drugs and alcohol, someone else will.
- Drugs and alcohol are part of our culture—your kids *will* be impacted by them.

- Even if you're a great parent, your children still might use drugs or alcohol.

CHAPTER 2

THE ALLURE

Why do children use drugs and alcohol?

In the previous chapter, as we considered reasons why you should speak with your children about drugs and alcohol, I think you must have begun to realize that being a prepared parent means being an educated parent. You don't have to become an expert on drugs and alcohol, and you certainly don't have to be able to qualify as a professional substance abuse educator, but you *do* have to know some basics about what drug or alcohol abuse could do to your children . . . and know how to talk to them about it effectively.

That's what *Talking Smack* does for you—it gives you the basics you need to know to protect your kids in this area of their lives. And let me tell you, it doesn't get any more basic, nor any more important, than the question we're going to consider right now: Why do children use drugs and alcohol?

What's the appeal of these substances?

More specifically, what might snag *your* kids into using them? (Or if they've already begun, what *did* snag them and why?)

These are the questions underlying a more important question that I bet you must be asking: *What can I say and do to take away the appeal of these dangerous substances for my children?*

In this chapter we'll discuss the top four reasons why kids use drugs and alcohol. And with each reason, I'll explain how you can help to protect your kids from the allure of these risky behaviors.

Peer Pressure—and the Desires That Lie behind It

When I'm speaking before groups of parents and ask the question that heads this chapter (Why do children use drugs and alcohol?), what do you suppose is the most common answer I get?

You're right: Peer pressure.

And that is a good answer. The first reason why kids use drugs and alcohol is *to be liked by their peers.* Our kids' friends are doing it and trying to talk our kids into doing it as well, so they go along. That's easy enough to understand.

But what most parents never consider is why peer pressure is so significant for our children, especially teens. I've discovered that peer pressure is so powerful because of two perfectly natural and normal desires that lie within our children.

The desire to belong to the group. Think about how important your own friendships are to you. Now multiply that feeling at least ten times over as you think about the intensity of the desire to belong for adolescents.

The reasons for this intensity are not hard to comprehend. Adolescents' bodies are undergoing enormous physical changes, and puberty is wreaking havoc with their self-image. This makes them extremely sensitive and vulnerable to what their peers think about them.

But let's delve deeper into this desire to belong and the factors that can counterbalance it. If we break it down, we see that there are many factors behind your child's ability to say no to drugs or alcohol in a pressure-cooker situation. Here are some of them:

- *Her status within the group.* Is she well liked, or is she struggling to establish herself within the group?
- *Her level of self-confidence.* Does she feel good about herself? Is she respected because of her abilities or achievements? Is she comfortable with her appearance?
- *A wide network of support.* If she is rejected by some of her peers, does she have the support of other friends? Does she have emotional support at home? Is home a safe place where she can talk about her challenges?

All these factors, which might seem unimportant to us, are supremely important to most teens. And they can have important results in the teens' lives.

Do you remember Melinda from the previous chapter—the girl who died after taking her first ecstasy pill? If you'll recall, Melinda came from a loving home where she had great parents. So why didn't she just say no when the pill was offered to her at the party?

I'm not sure what was going through Melinda's mind on that fateful night, but given the environment she was in, it would have been perfectly normal for her to feel pressure from her peers to go along with them in doing something risky. It would satisfy her need to be a part of the group. *What will my friends think of me if I don't try this pill?* she may have thought. *Would I be telling them I'm better than they are if I don't? What if I say no and they don't want me to be a part of their group anymore? I guess taking the drug is a small price to pay to belong.*

She took the drug. Sadly, for her, the price of attempting to belong could not have been steeper.

> What will my friends think of me if I don't try this pill? Melinda may have thought. Would I be telling them I'm better than they are if I don't?

A desire to be independent from parents. Another factor that contributes to adolescents' vulnerability to peer pressure relates to their desire to become less dependent on their parents. This, too, is normal and even healthy (within the right parameters). Children know as well as we do that they are on a journey toward being independent adults.

The problem is that the desire for this independence can often lead teens to engage in high-risk activities. By doing so, they are rebelling from the expectations of their parents in order to express their newfound independence and show others that they can handle more responsibility. Of course, for many adolescents, it is merely a charade—but it's a convincing one that causes parents much angst and frustration, placing a lot of stress on the relationship. Below the surface, their children may be experiencing much emotional turmoil with feelings of anxiety and fear of rejection by their peers, even though on the surface they exude confidence.

Some children, knowing full well that their parents don't want them to drink or use drugs, deliberately choose to do so as a way of proving that they are their own people. Peer pressure thus unites with a normal desire to produce unwanted behavior.

A Parent's Response to Peer Pressure

The times when your children are struggling with intense desires on the inside and powerful peer pressure on the outside are the times when your children need you the most. Avoid the temptation to let them go their own way. Stay involved in their lives.

Nothing appears to be worse for an adolescent than the rejection of her peers *and* her parents. Although extremely challenging, this is one season in your child's life when the love, understanding, patience, and forgiveness you provide as a parent is crucial for your child. She needs your help to survive those turbulent adolescent years. You may not feel like it, and your child may say she doesn't want it, but this is not the time to check out as a parent.

Is this easy? No! Parenting a teen will mean lying awake at night until your child comes home and you know she is okay. It will mean wondering whether you responded the right way or blew it. It will mean making the most of every opportunity to be there for your child, even when she says she doesn't need you, and being available when she says she does need you. Sometimes it will mean crying *with* her, and at other times it will mean crying *for* her.

> Sometimes parenting a teen will mean crying *with* her, and at other times it will mean crying *for* her.

There are also some practical things you can do to help your child resist peer pressure. Affirm her, build up her self-confidence by helping her to become good at something, and spend time with her so that you can better understand her world. Get to know her friends and the parents of her friends. Finally, become a fantastic listener—listen with your heart as well as your ears.

A friend of mine recently told me how his wife often goes to bed early in the evening so that she can get up when their teenage daughter comes home later that night. Although exhausted, she wants her child to know that she is important and that there will always be a listening ear when she comes home. It is not unusual for my friend's wife and daughter to talk into the early hours of the morning.

This is one girl who is less likely to make a bad choice about substance abuse.

"Get Me Out of Here!"

While peer pressure is a nearly universal factor in children's use of drugs and alcohol, there is another factor that is equally if not more powerful for some children. These young people use illicit substances as a way *to escape from unwanted*

Early Relationship Lessons

The desire to be liked and to have friends starts at a young age. From the early stages of children's social development, they have a strong need for affirmation and encouragement. This reinforces for the children what behavior is rewarded and liked by others as well as what behavior is detrimental to making friends.

In response to these dynamics, Natalie and I regularly let our three children know what we expect of them when they are around their friends. The following are the key characteristics we talk about often as we are in the car together or eating meals around the kitchen table:

- Be trustworthy.
- Respect yourself and others.
- Watch out for a friend who is left to play on his own or is told she can't be part of the group.
- Never give up.

These four characteristics have become a kind of unwritten family charter for us. Each of our kids knows that these characteristics are important to us as their parents. Equally, they know that having these characteristics will serve them well in life.

situations or transitions. Perhaps their home life is disruptive, their parents are constantly fighting, or they are suffering the pain of abuse or grief over the loss of someone or something important to them. It also might be a way to manage stress that comes from moving, changing schools, or trying to break into a new football team. Using drugs or alcohol can seem to these vulnerable children like a way to mask the pain and alleviate the stress.

Daniel was first referred to me as a thirteen-year-old homeless boy who was known for his violent outbursts and compulsive stealing of cars, which had come to the attention of the police. He had been placed in various homes and even incarcerated multiple times at a youth training center. He was described by his social worker as a "likeable maniac out of control."

It took a number of months for Daniel to trust me with his real story. Before that, his lies, colorful exploits, and exaggerated stories made it difficult for me to unravel what was really happening inside him and causing him to act out in these ways. In the end, though, I began to understand.

A couple of years earlier, when Daniel was eleven years old, his parents had finally separated after countless arguments and fights. Daniel was present during many of these outbursts, and he became increasingly anxious about his own welfare and feared that his family would break up.

He loved his mother and father, and it grieved him to see his parents not getting along. His inability to control what was happening led to pent-up frustration that would surface with outbursts of anger, which often preceded the exploits that were getting him into trouble with the law.

For almost a year, he survived on the streets, scrounging from friends what he needed to survive. In addition, he stole not only cars but also money, clothes, jewelry, and electronics—sometimes just for pleasure and at other times to get money to buy food. His survival kit eventually included the casual use of illicit drugs that would help him to mask his pain while giving him the bravado to maintain his exploits and reputation among his peers.

Although Daniel's story might sound extraordinary and be very different from your family situation, it highlights a desire that is real for all of us: the desire to avoid pain. For kids, just as for grown-ups, it is natural to want to escape suffering.

Being bullied at school, failing at sports, getting low grades, feeling insecure at home, finding it difficult to make friends, not liking the way they look—these are just some of the possible sources of pain in the lives of young people. And due to their immaturity and new hormones, their feelings of helplessness can sometimes not only fluctuate quickly from one extreme to the other but also accelerate to a point where things have blown out of all proportion in their mind. They might be willing to do almost anything to forget unwanted situations and feelings. That's when alcohol or drugs look appealing as a means of escape.

A Parent's Response to Escapism

Our reaction to our kids' pain should start with recognizing the reality of what they are feeling. We should never underestimate or play down the amount of pain they might be suffering or the intensity of their desire to escape that suffering. This means listening to our kids and learning about their world—their challenges and needs—without being judgmental.

In some cases, as we learn what they are going through, we may realize that there are ways we can help our children to safely reduce or eliminate the sources of pain in their lives. For example, if a child is feeling badly about how she looks, we can help her with advice about clothes, hairstyling, weight loss, or whatever she needs.

Of course, we will not always be able to "fix" the problems and worries in our kids' lives. But even then, with our greater maturity, we can give them a better perspective on what they are going through. If our son is distraught over the breakup of a teenage romance, for instance, we can help him see that he is still young and has plenty of time to find a girl who will love him.

Along with whatever practical help we can give our kids, we also can help them figure out the best way to react to the hurts in their lives. Resorting to drugs and alcohol as an escape is not the best solution. There are other ways of dealing with inner pain. With our consistent love and support, they can make these better choices.

Party Time!

We've already talked about peer pressure and a desire to escape pain as reasons why young people experiment with or use illegal substances. But here's another, much simpler reason: because *drugs and alcohol seem fun and helpful.*

We only have to look at how our culture celebrates significant sporting achievements and how our favorite television shows and movies legitimize the use of drugs and alcohol to understand why our children may perceive substance abuse as being fun. And there is no doubt that drugs do remove normal inhibitions, increase confidence levels, help people to relax, stimulate users to feel better about themselves, cause them to be more excited than they would otherwise be, and remove them from the discomfort and pain of an unwanted situation (albeit temporarily). It's no wonder that kids use drugs and alcohol to fuel the fun at parties.

And not only are drugs seen as fun but also performance-enhancing drugs can lure young people with the promise of success and reward. We sometimes forget this type of appeal to our children. Yet in our competitive culture, children are under much pressure from their teachers, coaches, peers, and parents to perform academically and athletically. Nobody wants to be a loser! As a result, performance-enhancing drugs have become a real issue for young people.

The example, of course, comes from the world of professional sports, where some of the world's best athletes have been banned from competition. Elaborate new schemes are devised and new concoctions of drugs are created to avoid detection. The message this sends to our children is this: "As long as you can get away with it, it's okay." So they try the performance-enhancing drugs too. Only later do they realize that any "success" the drugs give them comes at significant cost.

Even at a basic level, some young people drink copious amounts of coffee and take caffeine tablets that allow them to stay awake for long hours. This allows them to cram for their exams to avoid personal failure and to live up to high expectations.

For all of these reasons, using drugs and alcohol can seem like a good idea. The advantages seem obvious, while the dangers are more nebulous.

What's in a Name?

Attractive names are assigned to many illicit designer drugs as they come onto the market, making them appealing to young people. As examples, the following are four common drugs, each with multiple street names.

- *Cocaine*—aka "coke," "candy speedball," and so on.
- *Ecstasy*—aka "X," "E," "Versace," and so on. When ecstasy is used simultaneously with LSD, it is known as "candy flipping."
- *Meth* (methamphetamine)—aka "speed," "ice," "crystal ice," and so on.
- *Marijuana*—aka "pot," and so on. Marijuana cigarettes can include cocaine or be dipped in PCP and then are known as "happy sticks" or "love boat."

Sadly, the use of attractive names covers up the destructive effects of the drugs being used.

A Parent's Response to the Reputation of Drugs and Alcohol

As parents, we can understand why our children would want to experience the upside of drugs. Many parents think this phase will pass quickly and harmlessly and feel that there is not much they can do to steer their children away from it anyway. Herein lies the danger. Disengagement by a parent sends conflicting messages to the child.

You could be a part of the problem, instead of the solution, if you have said or thought anything like this:

- "She's just going through a passing phase."
- "A little bit of fun won't hurt him."
- "She needs to get it out of her system."
- "It never hurt me, so I'm sure he'll be okay."
- "She'll only learn if she learns the hard way, like I had to."
- "It's normal, adolescent risk-taking behavior."

So our first response must be to examine our own reaction to the appeal of drugs. Are we ourselves blinded to the dangers of substance abuse because of their superficial appeal? We need to maintain a consistent attitude of opposition to this behavior that can harm our kids.

Furthermore, because our children live in a world where drugs are readily available and glamorized, and because there is a growing acceptance of using drugs to help us feel better, parents need to look for opportunities to talk responsibly and truthfully to their children about drugs.

The "fun" reputation of drugs doesn't tell the whole story. We need to be reliable sources of information for our children so we can speak to them when opportunities arise.

What opportunities exist? Some might include the following:

- emphasizing the need for discipline and hard work to become good at something, reinforcing the fact that there are no shortcuts

- helping children set up a realistic schedule for themselves so that they don't have to stay awake cramming for exams
- helping children explore other ways to celebrate victories and being willing to model this
- exploring alternatives for dealing with stress and handling expectations

One day my two sons, Ben and Ryan, and I were watching television when a story came on about an NFL player who had gotten into trouble by using performance-enhancing drugs.

Ben asked, "Dad, what do steroids do?" (Actually, he pronounced it "steroods." He was only eight at the time.)

I replied, "They make you stronger and give you bigger muscles."

"What's wrong with that?" he responded.

I knew at once that this was a great opportunity for me to reinforce the consequences of using drugs with my sons. I put the TV on mute. And then for the next five minutes, while I carefully chose words that would make sense to these youngsters, we discussed how "sterood" use might make a player stronger but have negative effects on his body over the long haul, how it creates unfair competition because honest players who train hard without drugs might get less playing time, and how it damages the athlete's reputation and that of his sponsors.

"Wow, Dad," was Ben's response to the story we had seen. "He wanted to be the best. Now he's not even allowed to play! That was a stupid thing to do."

Lesson learned.

Children See, Children Do

Children are learning about their world and trying to figure out who they are. That's why they are so interested in, and affected by, how others behave. They have a tendency to want to copy the actions of others, especially people they like and admire. This is just as true when it comes to substance abuse as it is in other areas of life. *If he's drinking at the party, it must be all right,* our kids might think. Or, *If she's going to smoke the joint as it's passed around, then I will too.*

This gives us our final reason for why kids use drugs and alcohol: because *they see this kind of behavior being modeled.*

This modeling can come from actors or music artists the kids like. It can also come from the other young people your kids know at school or in the neighborhood. But perhaps most importantly, it can come from within the home.

Not long ago, Beverley attended a How to Drug Proof Your Kids program. For her, the most challenging part was the session that encouraged parents to examine their own attitudes, beliefs, and behavior to make sure that their words and actions did not conflict with the message they were trying to convey to their children.

As Beverley thought about it, she realized that on a typical day, after coming home from work, she would pour herself a glass of wine, plop herself in a comfortable chair, and say something like "Ah, that's better." Now it dawned on

It dawned on Beverley: even though she had *told* her children about the dangers of drug and alcohol abuse, she was *showing* them that it took a glass of wine to relieve the stress that had built up during the day.

her: even though she had *told* her children about the dangers of drug and alcohol abuse, she was *showing* them that it took a glass of wine to relieve the stress that had built up during the day.

Beverley started to wonder, would her actions contribute to her children seeing drugs or alcohol as a way out of the hardships in their life? What could she do to manage the stress in her life differently so that her actions would send a healthier message to her kids?

A Parent's Response to Children's Tendency to Copy Behavior

As parents, we can do only so much about the negative modeling that other people give our kids. We can, of course, pay attention to the models our children are exposed to and help them think through the implications of the choices others have made. We can also encourage them to be independent and have the courage to go against the flow when necessary.

At the same time, though, we need to consider how our own behavior might be making it difficult for our children to accept what we are saying. The example we set for our children makes a powerful impression. And if we are being hypocritical, our children (who are extremely perceptive, as I'm sure you know!) will see it and will likely react in a bad way.

We'll look at the importance of modeling healthy behavior for our children in more depth in chapter four. The important thing to remember at this point is simply that we can make our home the primary place where our children can see a safe lifestyle being lived out. This is one way we can take the shine off the allure of drugs and alcohol.

These substances have a powerful appeal for our kids. The more we understand this appeal, the more prepared we will be to help them see the other side—the danger these substances pose. And that's where we're going next.

Self-Evaluation

Can you think of some examples of when your child felt pressure to do something that was out of character? Did you use it as a teaching opportunity or discount it by convincing yourself that "it's just part of growing up"? How could you have handled it differently?

As you think about your child's growing need for independence, have you considered how you could create opportunities that communicate to him that you can see he is getting older and more responsible? This is a great way to be proactive. Make a list of some age-appropriate ways to facilitate this in your child. You might also want to list the ways you might be limiting your child's need for independence.

Take some time to consider whether the very things you are trying to teach to your child are contradicted by your own behavior. Does anything need to change?

Chapter 2 Summary

Reasons why children use drugs and alcohol—and your responses:

- *Reason 1:* To be liked by their peers. *Your response:* Stay involved in your kids' lives.

- *Reason 2:* To escape from unwanted situations or transitions. *Your response:* Take time to listen and learn about your children's world—their challenges and needs—without being judgmental.
- *Reason 3:* Because these substances seem fun and helpful. *Your response:* Be a reliable source of information for your children so you can speak responsibly and truthfully to them when opportunities arise.
- *Reason 4:* Because they see this kind of behavior modeled. *Your response:* Make sure that your own behavior is not sending conflicting messages.

CHAPTER **3**

THE BASICS

*How do I get started in talking with my children
about drugs and alcohol?*

By now you know that drugs and alcohol present an insidious threat to your children. And you know that *you* are the crucial element in preventing your children from suffering the harm that substance abuse can bring. Healthy communication at home is the best means of setting your children down the path to a promising future free of alcohol and drug abuse.

If I were teaching this material to a roomful of parents rather than writing it in a book, this is the point where I would expect a voice to pipe up in about the sixth row. "Excuse me," the voice would say. "I get what you've been saying, but I have a question: How do I get started in talking with my children about drugs and alcohol?"

And that would be a very good question. So in this chapter we'll be looking at some key guidelines that will get you going.

This will lay the groundwork for more specifics to come in the chapters that lie ahead.

Here you'll learn how to make conversations on this topic a regular component of your parent-child relationship. After all, teaching your children about the dangers of drugs and alcohol shouldn't be so much an event as a part of your normal conversation. To single out one exchange that makes you feel as though you've "done your duty" misses hundreds of opportunities to reinforce the importance of what you want your child to understand.

> Teaching your children about the dangers of drugs and alcohol shouldn't be so much an event as a part of your normal conversation.

One day a few months ago, I was in the car with my ten-year-old son, Ben, and we were creeping along on a highway past an accident site. Ben had never seen anything like the scene and was curious—and more than a little disturbed.

"How could something like that happen, Daddy?" he asked.

"Sometimes people are careless when they are driving," I answered. "They don't think properly and do silly things."

I was going to let the matter go at that. But then a light went on in my head.

I continued, "People do lots of different silly things. For example, drink too much beer or wine. That's not good for them and makes them do things they regret later on. Maybe the driver who caused this accident was drinking too much."

A little later in the conversation I mentioned that the legal age to drink where we live is twenty-one.

Ben asked, "Why do I have to be twenty-one years old to drink alcohol?"

I said, "Because people tend to be more responsible at that age than when they are younger. They don't drink just to be cool in front of their friends."

Just one little comment in the middle of a normal conversation. But added to a lot of other comments made over the years, it will help Ben to understand deep inside that he's better off not messing with drugs or drink.

Each of us should keep open lines of communication with our children and, wherever appropriate, work in messages about drugs and alcohol. That kind of conversation comes naturally as part of healthy relationships and in turn helps to build healthy relationships.

But it all starts with having the right determination.

The Power of Saying, "I Will!"

You make intentional, responsible decisions every day. You might decide to set the alarm clock before you go to sleep at night so that you can get to work on time. You might decide to give up your daily latte so that you can save money for the new car your family needs.

And you're just as intentional and responsible when it comes to your role as a parent. You might restrict the television your children are permitted to

In the same way you make deliberate choices each day about routine things, so you need to decide to prepare your children for what they will face in regard to drugs and alcohol.

watch. You might check to make sure they are doing their homework.

Well, consider this: In the same way you make deliberate choices each day about routine things, so you need to decide to prepare your children for what they will face in regard to drugs and alcohol. The simple point I want you to remember is that you need to *be intentional*.

From the moment your children reach an age where they are observing everything around them, interpreting and storing that data for future decisions, you must make a conscious decision to get involved in the lives of your children. Think carefully about the information and values you want to teach your children. Choose to talk to them in ways that will be of help to them later on.

We'll be getting to the *what* and the *how* of starting communication with your children a bit later. But before that we have to consider the *when*.

Never Too Early

One day Tony, a father I had been talking to, asked me, "When would be the best time to begin talking to my children about drugs?" Although his children were still preschoolers, he didn't want to miss the opportunity to teach his kids before they began to be influenced by others around them.

Tony was open to the idea that conversations about drugs and alcohol should begin when children are young. Unfortunately, I have met many other parents who have waited to discuss the topic until their children are in high school. That's a mistake. True, it's better late than never. But it's best early than late.

I strongly recommend that you don't let your children reach the turbulent adolescent years while still in ignorance about the risks of alcohol and drug abuse. You should be communicating reliable information about drinking and drugs as soon as possible, even in your children's preschool years.

Would you wait until your child is past puberty to discuss with him the realities and responsibilities of sex? Would you wait until your child turns sixteen and drives the family car onto the highway to teach him how to drive? No, of course not. And neither should you let your child get to the point of greatest vulnerability to drugs and alcohol before presenting the topic in the way you want your child to learn it.

Here's the key when it comes to discussing drugs and alcohol with your child: *start early and stick with it.*

Of course, you have to communicate at an age-appropriate level. For example, if you were to suddenly start talking to a six year old about the dangers of heroin, it would be beyond her ability to comprehend. But you could help her understand that smoking cigarettes is not healthy and causes people to get sick. This would help her start thinking about taking care of her body by choosing carefully what she puts in it.

Age-appropriateness also applies to the way you go about communicating. Sitting your nine-year-old child down in front of you and giving him a thirty-minute lecture is not the best way to get your message across. Not only will he not appreciate the significance of your message, but also your misusing an opportunity to talk to your child will make it harder for him to listen to you next time. Briefer messages worked nonthreateningly into everyday conversations will work better for this boy.

We'll be looking at age-appropriate conversation in much more depth in future chapters. But the thing to remember at this point is that, as parents, we need to anticipate the challenges and needs of our children before they arrive at the most critical juncture of attraction to drugs and alcohol. And we need to get started right away.

Understanding the individual situation each of our children faces will help us know what to do.

Factor This In

In recent years there has been a significant amount of research highlighting both risk factors and protective factors for young people regarding decisions they might make in critical areas of life, including whether to use drugs or alcohol.[2] The fact is, every child has a mix of risk factors as well as protective factors in his or her life. These determine the potential threat of drugs and alcohol entering a child's life. Let's take a look at both kinds of factors and why it is helpful for you to understand how they interact in your child's life.

Risk factors. These are things that put a child at risk of making poor decisions or engaging in unhealthy behaviors. Risk factors for children include:

- low self-esteem
- inability to respond appropriately to negative pressure from peers
- lack of information to help them make wise decisions
- learning difficulties at school and low grades
- unhealthy relationship with a parent
- being bullied at school
- stressful home environment

When factors such as the ones listed above touch a child's life, that child is much more at risk of making a poor decision in regard to drinking and drug use. Add to this mounting pressure from his peers, and it becomes even tougher for a child to make the right decision.

Therefore, as a parent, one of your top priorities must be to try to minimize the presence of these risk factors, better preparing your child for the challenges he'll face as he moves into adolescence and beyond.

Protective factors. These are things that help children achieve developmental milestones relative to their age and therefore be more resilient when negative influences appear. Some protective factors include the following:

- building your child's self-esteem
- helping your child to develop strong interpersonal skills

Tips for Building Protective Factors

Consider these practical ways you can be intentional in building protective factors into your child's life:

- Sit down together for meals as a family.
- Go on monthly outings or activities where the whole family can participate.
- Support your child as he or she strives to fulfill a dream.
- If you have more than one child, ensure that you are dividing your time fairly between your children and in pursuing what is of interest to each of them.
- Plan one-on-one time with your kids and let them choose the activity. This is a great time to focus on appreciating something they enjoy doing. You might be surprised at what you'll learn!
- Create a supportive, affirming home environment. Encouraging words, rather than critical barbs, get much better results. Hugs, kisses, play wrestling, and a pat on the shoulder communicate to children that they are special to you. The last thing your child needs from you is the knowledge that she will never be good enough or measure up to the expectations you have for her.
- Show a united front with your spouse when it comes to reinforcing boundaries

and consequences so that your children can see this is something you have discussed and agreed on together. Children are masters when it comes to playing one parent off against the other.

- giving your child a loving and supportive home environment
- setting healthy boundaries and reinforcing consequences
- encouraging your child to get involved in recreational activities

Although children with more risk factors are at risk of engaging in drug use or other problem behaviors, it doesn't mean they will automatically engage in high-risk activities. The presence of protective factors can balance and buffer the risk factors.

At a time when your child may be going through many changes and stresses, building these protective factors into your home life and relationship with your child will help her to be stronger when facing the challenges of adolescence. That's why it's important to understand and respond to the factors that are influencing your child.

And that's still not all. I've saved the most important truth for last.

Reasons for Educating Yourself

Parents who want their children to listen to them must be able to deliver a message with credibility. Older children, in particular, will know it if their parents are talking about something they don't really understand. And even if children don't realize at the time that they are being told inaccurate information, they certainly will later on as they become more informed by experience or their peers.

> Lori shared how her mother had tried to discourage her from smoking marijuana by telling her that her hair would fall out if she did.

One day when I was speaking in a classroom, a girl named Lori shared how her mother had tried to discourage her from smoking marijuana by telling her that her hair would fall out if she did. Lori blurted out, "If that was true, then half my class would have no hair!" The entire class burst into laughter.

What a mistake Lori's mom made by inventing this false "fact"! She had found a sure-fire way of losing credibility with her child.

And that is why my next guideline is *know your stuff.* You have to educate yourself about the different kinds of drugs and alcohol as well as the effects of those substances on the human body.

The good news is that today there are many books a parent can purchase to learn about the range of drugs available to their children, the different names used for drugs, and what effect they may have on a young person. The Internet is also an invaluable resource for parents seeking more information. (See the appendix for resources you can use.)

As you educate yourself about drugs and alcohol, you will feel more capable when talking to your child about the issue. And when you feel this way, you will be better able to reason with your child, gently correct her perspective if it is based on untrue information, and increase her confidence in you.

Other reasons for knowing the facts about drugs and alcohol include the following:

It will enable you to take advantage of opportunities that arise. Remember the saying "A scout is always prepared"? The same should be true for you.

There will be times when you have unexpected opportunities to talk to your child about drugs. More than likely you won't be able to excuse yourself from the conversation because you want to research the Internet for information. Not being ready with reliable and relevant information will result in a missed opportunity to be a positive influence in the life of your child.

It will make your children more open to listening to you. Your child is more likely to listen to you because what you are saying is trustworthy. You'll get the hearing you want.

Already I can hear you saying that evidently I don't know how temperamental your child can be. He or she won't listen no matter how reliable your information is!

It's true that nothing, not even having accurate information, surpasses the importance of having a strong and healthy relationship with your child. However, when your child is finally in a place to hear you, at least you will know that the information you are sharing with your child is reliable.

It will help you to be more objective and less reactive. The more you know about drinking and drugs, the more rational you can be in talking to your child about them. You'll be less tempted to explode out of anger, fear, or frustration.

Engaging in a battle of words with your child, or becoming irrational, will cause you to lose influence on your child's decisions. That's the last thing you want.

It will show your child that you care. There are evenings when I come home from work tired and flop into the lounge chair to watch some meaningless television so that I don't have to think. When bedtime comes, I hustle the kids into bed, telling them that it's too late to read them a story. (What that means is, the commercial break is almost over!) I turn toward the door, only to hear "Daddy, we forgot to say our prayers." (Now I'm thinking, *The commercial break is finished and I'm going to miss some crucial part of the program I was watching.*)

So I know what it's like. We parents are often so tired that just getting ourselves and our kids through the day seems like an achievement. And yet—believe me—they know when we aren't paying them the attention they deserve.

That's why when you educate yourself on the subject, making an effort to understand your child's world and how illegal substances can harm it, your child will take notice. Most of the time, when we make an effort with our kids, they benefit from the investment we have made.

You will become aware of resources that can help you. Taking the time to learn what you need to know about drugs and alcohol invariably means talking to other parents, teachers, coaches, and pastors. You never know when you might find an ally in your efforts, and that's a wonderfully reassuring thing.

We see this all the time in the How to Drug Proof Your Kids program. One of the first observations made during the program is the overwhelming relief felt by parents as they realize that other parents are as concerned as they are about the lurking danger of drugs for their children. They begin to see that the parents have more to contribute to each other than they thought prior to beginning the program.

In a beautiful way, parents seeking information and practical skills for themselves become a resource and support to each other. And this is only one of many great reasons to be sure you know what you're talking about when you discuss drugs and alcohol with your kids. But just as important as having the right information is knowing how to use it.

Rules for an Effective Conversation

Remember, I said that talking with your kids about the dangers of drugs and alcohol should be an ongoing conversation with them. My last guideline for you, then, is this: *plan for an effective conversation.* That is, think about what kind of communication will get your message across effectively and always leave the door open for further conversations.

Below are some tips to help you maximize opportunities to engage your child in conversation.

Keep it private. We all remember at least one time from our childhood when our parents enraged us by sharing something embarrassing about us in front of our siblings or friends. It wasn't the right time or place for that kind of communication. One principle I have tried to put into practice with my colleagues at work is also one I try to apply at home: Affirm in public, rebuke in private.

Likewise, as our own children get older, they become extremely self-conscious and sensitive to what we say when their friends are around. If we fail to recognize this, we can be armed with the best information and it still won't hit the target or get the result we are looking for. That's why we need to wait for those moments when we have our children to ourselves to bring up the sensitive subject of substance abuse.

Seize teachable moments. Sometimes you may have to create an opportunity to talk with your kids about this subject. But if you're paying attention, you will also find that occasionally events occur that naturally lend themselves to conversations about alcohol and drugs. Your daughter informs you that someone offered her a shot to drink at a party. Your son's sports hero is fined for doping. (Remember my "steroods" conversation with my sons?)

If an opportunity arises for you to constructively address the issue of drugs and alcohol with your child, don't put it off, thinking that you will raise the issue later. Seize the moment! Another opportunity like the one you have now may be a long time in coming. Better to say something now than to regret not having said it and see your child suffer the consequences.

Don't underestimate the power of context and timing in getting your message through to your child.

Be sensitive to your child's needs. You want the conversation to be constructive. So make sure you conduct it in a way that is as comfortable as possible for a child.

For example, you don't want to pick an awkward time for the conversation. Ask yourself whether this will be the time when your child will be most responsive to what you want to discuss. Is he in a hurry? Is he distracted by something else? Is he under stress or pressured by homework or exams? Is he tired?

Make sure it's a two-way conversation. Let's be honest. There are few things so deadening as being cornered in a one-way conversation where all you can do is listen and hope that you don't have to endure it too long. Similarly, imagine how your child feels when you're the one doing the cornering!

It is important to give your child an opportunity to ask questions without having to fear judgment or have you constantly interrupt and tell him he shouldn't think that way. Encourage him to open up and share his thoughts and how he is feeling about what you are saying. It helps to reinforce the message you want him to hear. What may appear to be straightforward to you may not be so clear to him.

Ask open-ended questions. Ever tried to have a discussion with someone and all you got were one-word responses to your questions—"Yes," "No," "Maybe"? (If you have a teenager, you could probably add that these responses are interspersed with the occasional grunt!)

To make the conversation more meaningful for you and your child, think of how you can ask questions that require your child to think and engage with you. Open-ended questions often start with words like *who, what, when, how,* or *why.* Try questions like these with your children:

- "How did that make you feel?"
- "Why do you think they did that?"
- "What other options might there have been?"
- "What do you think would have been the result?"
- "What do you think you would do differently next time?"

Admit it when you're stumped. It is easy to be caught off guard by a question from your child that you are unsure how to answer. Rather than stumble through an awkward and incorrect response, it is better for you to acknowledge that you don't know the answer and promise that you will look for information and talk about it again later.

Using Words Wisely

1. When was the last time I sat down and had a meaningful and unhurried conversation with my child?

2. Do I have a tendency to criticize my child in front of others?

3. What words have the greatest positive impact on my child? When was the last time I used those words?

4. Have I been sharing my time with each of my children or been too focused on one?

5. Do I really listen to my child, or have I tended to dominate conversations?

This and the other guidelines for an effective conversation can help you make the most of the conversations you have with your kids about drugs and alcohol. After all, your goal is not to check off another parenting task completed. It is to really influence your child's perspective on drugs and alcohol over time.

Over time—that is indeed how our conversations with our kids about this subject must take place. As I said earlier, we need to start early with our kids and then stick with it.

Of course, there are obvious differences in the intellectual capacity and social maturity of a child in preschool or elementary school compared to those of a child who is seemingly sprinting through adolescence toward young adulthood. For this reason, I have set aside the next few chapters to talk about principles for making our conversations appropriate for kids of different ages.

Chapter 3 Summary

Guidelines for getting started in talking with your children about drugs and alcohol:

- Be intentional—make the responsible decision to address drugs and alcohol with your kids regularly.
- Start early and stick with it—discuss the topic beginning in the preschool years and continuing as long as your kids are under your roof.
- Understand risk and protective factors—know and influence the substance abuse threat level in your children's lives.

- Know your stuff—be sure that you have reliable, up-to-date information to share with your kids.
- Plan for an effective conversation—follow the rules for good communication.

CHAPTER 4

FOR PARENTS OF YOUNGER CHILDREN

How do I protect my preschooler or elementary-age child from drugs and alcohol?

So far, we've looked at the important role parents play in protecting their children from drugs and alcohol, the powerful appeal these substances have for young people, and what it takes to begin having effective discussions with children. Now we need to get more specific.

As I have said, discussing substance abuse is not an event; it is a journey where the messages your child hears from you are reinforced hundreds of times within the context of a loving, affirming relationship. And as I have also said, these conversations should ideally be taking place throughout the years your child is at home. So, what do you say and do at different stages of your child's life?

> Discussing substance abuse is not an event; it is a journey.

The greatest risk posed by illegal substances usually comes in the teen years, and I assure you that we'll be getting to how to talk to older children in a chapter soon to come. But just as important is getting the subject out there with your kids while they are younger. If your kids are in grade school or even younger, you can begin now to talk to them about the dangers of substance abuse in an age-appropriate way, laying the groundwork for a lifetime of wise choices in this area.

> If your kids are in grade school or even younger, you can begin now to talk to them about the dangers of substance abuse in an age-appropriate way, laying the groundwork for a lifetime of wise choices in this area.

In this chapter we'll be looking at three key guidelines. As you read about each one, think about your young children and how you can follow these guidelines naturally and effectively in your own home.

And one other thing. At times, as you work your way through this chapter, it may seem as though I'm getting away from the topic of this book. But hang in there with me. I assure you that each of the guidelines you'll find here is a key to good parenting and particularly to protecting your kids from dangerous substances. I think you'll see by the end how it all fits together.

The first guideline we'll consider is the most basic of all: *Talk about healthy living and model it.*

You First

You've heard the saying "Values are caught, not taught." And it's true. Our kids watch what we do—that is, how we live out what we believe—and then imitate us.

You may remember Beverley from chapter two. She was the mom who had a drink every day after work to unwind—or at least she did until she thought about the message this practice was sending to her kids. That's a negative example about how values are "caught."

But the good news is that positive values can be catching as well. As we choose to eat well, exercise, get adequate rest, seek medical care when needed, and refuse to use drugs or alcohol as emotional crutches, our children will see all of that and learn a better way to live. Research overwhelmingly supports the fact that when parents model a healthy lifestyle for their children, their children are more likely to follow in their footsteps.[3] If we want our children to have a healthy respect for themselves, their bodies, and those around them, then we will think carefully about the attitudes and behaviors we model at home.

I vividly recall a stressful time in my life when, over a period of about six months, I was having frequent headaches. As a result, I was constantly taking pain medication. I didn't even really think about it—I just took the pills.

Now, there was nothing *illegal* about my taking these pills. But there was something *unwise* about it.

You see, I finally began to realize some things. I realized that it was not healthy for me to be on a regular diet of medication if I did not have to be. I also realized that using painkillers meant that I wasn't dealing with the underlying issue of stress.

And just as importantly, I realized that my response to my headache problem was setting a bad example for my children. They were watching me pop those pills.

I had to make some lifestyle changes, and I did. For me, that meant starting to eat breakfast again, rather than skipping it and then giving in to a midmorning craving for chocolate and a can of Coke. It meant trying to maintain a better exercise routine (something that I am still not always successful with, alas!). And it meant making sure I added some escapist novels to my reading list rather than just focusing on books with a professional development edge.

These changes were simple. But they lowered the level of stress in my life to a point where the headaches went away—and the painkillers went back in the medicine cabinet. My kids saw that, too.

Paying attention to the behaviors we are modeling is important. But I have found that the "caught, not taught" outlook is true only up to a point. You actually *can* teach values . . . as long as you are at the same time modeling those values. Your behavior gives your words credibility. So go ahead—work in spoken messages along with the unspoken ones about healthy living for your children.

What are the key messages our children need to hear from us? Here are some:

- "You are special."
- "We care about you."
- "We want to help you make good decisions."
- "Decisions have consequences."
- "A healthy diet and exercise are good for you."

- "What you eat and drink sometimes changes the way you feel."
- "We set boundaries to protect you from getting hurt."
- "Being healthy will help you to do better at sports."

So let me get personal for a moment. What are *you* saying to your children about healthy living? And what is the way you are living saying to them? As you help them see the value of healthy living, you will be forming a pattern in their lives that will help them to resist poor choices about drugs and alcohol later in life.

Talk about it. Live it! What better way to give your child a good start in life?

This is the starting point. But we've got another guideline to consider. And as a way of getting at it, let me introduce you to a mom and son whose story may remind you of some things that take place in your own home.

> Talk about it. Live it! What better way to give your child a good start in life?

Tina and Jack

Tina was bringing in another load of grocery bags from the car when she stopped in horror, seeing what her second grader, Jack, was holding in his hand as he sat at the kitchen counter.

"Jack!" she shouted. "Put that down!"

Jack stared at her wide-eyed, a handful of painkillers in his hand.

Tina remembered now: before heading out to the supermarket with her son, she had taken a couple of pills from that bottle to try to get rid of a pounding headache. She must have neglected to put the lid back on tightly.

Now she hurriedly scooped the pills out of Jack's hand and slipped them back into the bottle. She made sure the lid was on securely this time.

Jack started to whimper, not understanding what had just happened.

Tina hugged him. When he was feeling better, she began to explain.

"Jack, I'm so sorry I yelled at you like that," said Tina. "But that wasn't candy you were about to put in your mouth. They were tablets that your dad and I take when we have a bad headache. They could have hurt you a lot."

Jack sighed in relief, realizing that he was not in trouble. But with a puzzled look, he said to his mother, "If they help you and Dad get better, how come the tablets would hurt me?"

Tina thought carefully about how to answer. She began, "Jack, you've seen me bake a cake before, haven't you?"

"Yeah, lots of times," replied Jack.

"A cake is made up of lots of different things, such as eggs, flour, sugar, milk, and nuts. These are called ingredients."

Jack nodded his head in agreement.

She continued, "Sometimes I've tried to bake a cake and it hasn't turned out. Usually that's because I forgot one important ingredient or I didn't use the correct amount mentioned in the recipe book.

"Well, medicine is also made up of different ingredients, and depending on how old you are and what is wrong with you, some medicines work better than others. If you take medicine that is not meant for you, or the wrong amount of what you need, then the medicine could even cause you to get sick."

Jack looked serious and asked Tina, "Does that mean I could have died today?"

Tina replied, "I don't know. You might have gotten sick if you swallowed too many tablets. That's why it's very important to only eat things you know are good for you or what the doctor gives you when you are sick. If you're not sure, come and ask me or your father."

How to Protect Children from Dangerous Household Products

- Do an inventory check of potentially dangerous substances in the house and either remove them or relocate them.
- Be especially careful with medication. Discard unused or expired medications.
- When appropriate, remind your kids that while medicines can help people to get better, the wrong medicine can cause people to get sick or even die.
- Create teachable moments about household safety while your children are still young.

"Sure, Mom," replied Jack. "Of course I will." Then he ran off to play.

It was Tina's turn to sigh in relief. She had made a careless mistake—one that could have resulted in a parent's worst nightmare. But she hoped that Jack had learned the lesson she had taught. It might protect him in the future.

Safe at Home

As Jack learned, many substances in a typical house are dangerous to children. Teaching your children about these things when they are young, even before kindergarten, can serve as a helpful platform as they approach adolescence and face new challenges in middle and high school. The key to remember, then, is this: *Protect your children from, and educate them about, dangerous household substances.*

Let's take an inventory of potentially dangerous substances (especially when swallowed by little children) that can easily be found in most homes. The degree of danger is obviously related to the dosage levels and whether they are used inappropriately. For example, vitamins and prescribed medication are safe when used properly, but when ingested in large quantities or for reasons other than what is recommended, they can cause significant damage—even death in some cases. Most of these substances typically reside in the laundry, bathroom, and garage, but some can be found in the kitchen. These include:

- Bleach/disinfectant
- Laundry detergent
- Toilet cleaner
- Fabric softener
- Window cleaner

- Carpet stain remover
- Dishwasher capsules
- Nail polish remover
- Painkillers
- Lawn fertilizer
- Paint thinner
- Gasoline
- Weed killer
- Prescription medication
- Vitamins
- Cough medicine
- Alcohol
- Tobacco
- Caffeine

There's nothing profound about this list, and it certainly doesn't include all the different chemicals you may have in your house. But each of them can pose a threat to your children.

And if your children show an interest in these products, you have a chance to tell them about making wise choices regarding substances they might ingest. Like Tina, you'll have a chance to teach a lesson. Here is the key: in much the same way that you talk to your young child about the danger of these things to steer him away from being hurt, you are laying the foundation for further substance abuse education with your child when he grows older. After all, drugs are chemicals.

This leads us to our third and final guideline for protecting younger children from harmful substances. I've got another story for you.

Conversation Starters to Use with Your Elementary-Age Child

Ready to talk to your kid about drugs and alcohol? Great! Below are some questions to get the conversation rolling. Note that they start with relationship-building questions and move to questions that are more specifically related to drugs and alcohol.

- "Who is your best friend and why? What do you look for in a friend?"
- "If you could do anything you wanted when you become older, what would that be?
- "What is your greatest fear?"
- "What's the most embarrassing thing that has ever happened to you at school or while you were with friends?"
- "If you could change one thing about our family, what would that be?"
- "What makes you really angry? What makes you really happy?"
- "What was the best thing that happened to you today? What was the worse thing?"
- "If you could choose anywhere to go for a family vacation, where would it be?"
- "Do you know what drugs and alcohol are? Do you know why they are bad for you?"

- "Have you ever seen someone who was drunk or high on drugs? How did you feel about that?"
- "What should you do if someone offers you alcohol to drink or a pill to take?"
- "What questions do you have for me about drugs or alcohol?"

David and Susan

"Susan, turn that music down!" yelled David to his ten-year-old daughter.

Unable to hear himself think as he attempted to scan the sports pages, David had had enough of his daughter's noise. Five minutes after excusing herself from the dinner table, Susan had gone to her room, shut the door, and turned up the volume on her MP3 player.

It seemed like every night was becoming a battle between David and his daughter. Lately it had gotten so bad that he had even begun to dread pulling into the garage after work, anticipating what he was about to walk into. Tonight he thought, *I need try something different.*

David called his good friend Gary—the father of four teenagers—to see if Gary could provide some much-needed wisdom. David had seen how close Gary was to his children and knew that he must have faced some parenting battles along the way.

Gary explained that what had helped him and his wife meet some of the challenges with their four children was implementing what he called "the cause-and-effect principle."

This wise friend explained to David, "I made sure that my expectations for my children were realistic and were very clear to them. Then I gave them a choice: to do what they knew I wanted from them or not. They knew that if they chose to disregard what I expected from them, there would be consequences."

"And did you follow through on the consequences when they misbehaved?" asked David.

"Oh yes. Of course, there were times when this broke my heart. One time I kept my son home from a summer camp that he had been looking forward to for months. But I knew that if my kids didn't grow up with a clear sense of responsibility for their behavior and decisions, I would have failed them as a father."

Wow! thought David. *Why have I never seen this connection so clearly before?*

Gary continued, "Before and after implementing the consequence, and sometimes even during the consequence, I would calmly talk to my children about why they were experiencing this. I helped them to understand how things could have been different if they had made a better decision. I also used this time to affirm what I liked about them and how I saw them growing."

Gary gave David one other important tip that reminded David he was in a parenting partnership with his wife. "Be in agreement with Lisa. You and Lisa can't afford to contradict each other on the cause-and-effect principle; otherwise, you'll send conflicting messages to your children."

As he hung up the phone that night, David began to think about how he and his wife could apply the cause-and-effect principle in their own home. *What things could we try with Susan? What consequences would be appropriate for a ten year old?*

David began to smile. He realized things were going to be different, perhaps not immediately, but certainly in time. He couldn't wait to share with Lisa the wisdom Gary had shared with him.

How to Implement the Cause-and-Effect Principle with Children

- Establish realistic expectations for your children as well as appropriate consequences for violations of those expectations.
- Make sure your children understand both the expectations and the consequences.
- If your children violate your expectations, let them experience the consequences just as you had warned them.
- Teach and affirm them during the experience.
- Be sure that both parents are consistent in communication, expectations, and the delivery of consequences.

Establishing Consequences

Gary's cause-and-effect principle introduces my next point: *we need to help our children learn that decisions have consequences.* They must learn that if they choose to do A, then B will follow. We should never hide from them the natural consequences of their behavior, nor should we protect them from those consequences if doing so would weaken their sense of responsibility. Sometimes we all have to learn the hard way.

Some consequences for bad behavior are out of our control. A parent can warn an active third grader not to jump off a high retaining wall, but if he chooses to do it anyway, he could wind up with a sprained ankle that keeps him inactive for days. It's a shame he has to experience the pain of his injury, and the parent would like to have spared him, but this can be a learning experience in itself.

And then there are the consequences we deliberately set up for our children. I'm talking about punishment for violating expectations we establish for our kids. Consistently applied discipline for violating these expectations can be an invaluable means of teaching our children to keep themselves under control.

Of course, when it comes to the consequences we set up for violation of the expectations we establish for our kids, we have to make sure they are appropriately matched to the decisions. We probably wouldn't ground a teenager for a month for taking the family car out without

> Appropriately assigned and consistently implemented consequences will help children take responsibility for their actions.

permission. But we might keep the car keys from him for a week.

Also, we need to keep in mind a distinction: the consequences we establish for our children should serve as an *unpleasant reminder* of the importance of taking responsibility for one's actions; they should never result in *actual harm*. It may be perfectly appropriate for a child who has done wrong to feel some hurt pride, undergo a loss of privileges, or be required to pay money to replace something she broke. But we should never harm her through physical injury, abandonment, or any other punishment that would result in emotional damage such as anxiety, stress, fear, or depression.

Appropriately assigned and consistently implemented consequences will help children take responsibility for their actions. And this is a lesson they can and should learn from an early age. Even preschoolers can begin taking ownership of their decisions in many areas of life.

You may have noticed that David's flashpoint with his daughter, Susan, had nothing to do with drugs or alcohol. And indeed most of our disciplinary situations with our children won't. But ingraining the message about consequences in our children will bear wonderful fruit when later they are invited to drink a beer or smoke a joint or pop a pill. Compared to other kids, they will be more likely to stop and think, *What will I be doing to myself if I choose to do this?*

This is such an important topic that we need to consider it at more length. You see, expectations are just one part of a bigger issue—an issue that is crucial from the time they are young and continuing throughout their time at home. I'm talking about the issue of setting boundaries.

Chapter 4 Summary

Guidelines for protecting your preschooler or elementary-age child from drugs and alcohol:

- Talk about healthy living and model it.
- Protect your children from, and educate them about, dangerous household substances.
- Help your children learn that decisions have consequences.

A SAFE PLACE

How do I set healthy boundaries for my children?

I've noticed a curious thing when I talk to parents about protecting their kids from drugs and alcohol: the conversation almost always comes around to the issue of establishing boundaries for children. It's as if our parenting instinct unerringly guides us toward the context within which we can best teach our kids about substance abuse.

Wouldn't you say that our ultimate goal is to help our children make the right choices *on their own* about drinking and taking drugs? I would. And so there has to be something inside the kids that shows them what those right choices are. This means they have to have a clear sense of the boundry between right and wrong.

The way they learn about right and wrong in every area of life, not just drugs, is through the boundaries we set for their behavior while they are still in our homes. We establish boundaries for our children when they are young so that they will establish—and stick to—boundaries for themselves when they are older.

Boundary setting is something that parents ought to be practicing from the time their children are small and throughout adolescence. So whether your child is looking forward to kindergarten or starting to look into colleges, effective boundary setting is a skill you need.

Most of us parents "get" this deep down inside. But the reason my conversations with parents drift into this topic so often is that so many of us aren't sure exactly how to establish and manage boundaries with our children. You, yourself, may be wondering, *How do I set healthy boundaries for my child?*

That is what we're going to learn in this chapter. Before that, though, I think we had better ask a more basic question: What do we mean by "boundaries" in the first place? For this, I'd like to tell you a story from my own life.

Inside the Fence

In 2004, while my family was living in Australia, I embarked on a project to build a picket fence at the front of our house. We lived on a street that provided access to a school and nearby playground and that sometimes became extremely busy. Monday through Friday, mornings and afternoons, cars would seemingly come from nowhere as parents arrived to either drop off their children for school or pick them up once school had finished. At that stage we had a nine-month-old son, Ben, and an expectation that he would not be our only child. (Ryan arrived a year later.) We felt that a fence would provide some added protection and freedom for Ben as he played.

Now, I have to admit that I am not the most practical man you could ever meet. My children would go hungry if they depended on my skills as a handyman to earn a living. Fortunately, after having enlisted the help of my capable father, I was able to complete the project (albeit four months after having started!).

Finally Ben, now having celebrated his first birthday, could crawl (and eventually run) around freely, and do what little boys do, without his mother having to constantly keep watch so that he wouldn't run out onto the street. Having that fence was a way of showing Ben what area was safe to play in. And we, as parents, no longer had to worry about Ben wandering out onto the road and getting hurt.

Ben, and eventually Ryan, had freedom to play within the designed parameters. But that freedom came with responsibility and consequences. If they climbed over the fence or opened the gate without Natalie or myself being present or without our permission, then they had overstepped the boundary. We often reminded them when they were young that the boundary was set to protect them and to stop them from getting hurt. What they learned, even from this young age, was that their choices would result in consequences. They could enjoy the freedom or run the risk of getting hurt.

That picket fence was a physical boundary. But it also represented a behavioral boundary, indicating what our boys were expected to do. All children need such boundaries.

A boundary is essentially a protective measure put in place by parents to keep their children safe and teach them responsibility.

A boundary is essentially a protective measure put in place by parents to keep their children safe and teach them responsibility. When a child ignores or oversteps a boundary, that child can expect to experience consequences that discourage this type of behavior from happening again. As we learned in the last chapter, sometimes these consequences are the natural result of the unwanted behavior and sometimes they are punishments the parents impose to make sure that the child learns a lesson. Often they are both.

The key is to introduce boundaries into our child's life at an early stage and keep adjusting them over the years to keep them relevant and appropriate for our child at any age. When they are young, we teach our children to keep away from a hot iron, to look both ways before crossing the road, and to be respectful of others' property. Later they need boundaries about staying out late, keeping up with schoolwork, and going on dates.

As a matter of fact, there are many types of boundaries touching every area of life.

Examples of Boundaries

Boundaries impact our children's relationships at home, school, and church. They help them to manage their emotions, keep their relationships healthy, and stay safe in a dangerous world. They *need* boundaries. That's why we should never forget the principle that *parents should set reasonable boundaries, with appropriate consequences, for key areas of their children's behavior.*

Let's take a look at some of those key areas and the kinds of boundaries parents might establish for them.

Self-Directed Questions for Boundary Setters

- What are age-appropriate boundaries for my children?
- When was the last time I reviewed the boundaries I have set to see if they are still age-appropriate?
- Is it possible that my expectations for my children are not clear to them? If so, what steps could I take to change this?
- Do I give my children the ability to influence the boundaries I set and agree on what the consequences might be?
- Am I consistent in allowing my children to experience the appropriate consequences for their behavior?
- When my children are experiencing the consequences of their behavior, do I express empathy with them?
- When was the last time I sat down with my children to talk about whether the consequences were fair? And did I really listen to them?

Communication. Mom and Dad will not discuss an issue with a child while he is yelling at them, crying, or complaining.

Finances. Mom and Dad refuse to buy a child the latest video game, because she could have saved for it instead of spending all of her pocket money.

Property. Children borrow someone else's property with the understanding that, if it they lose or break it, they will have to replace it.

School. The parents agree that the kids can wake themselves up in the morning. But if they are late for school, they will have go to bed one hour earlier so that they are not as tired in the morning.

Television. In order to stop the arguing over what program to watch on television, each child in the family will be given a day of the week to choose what the family watches. No other TVs will be turned on. Any child who does not wish to watch what is on can do something else instead.

If you tried, you could easily think up other areas of life where your children need boundaries, I'm sure. But right now I'd like to ask you some questions: Do you see how, if a family has boundaries like these in all kinds of significant areas of life, the children will be more willing to respect boundaries relating to drugs and alcohol? And do you see how, as children get used to boundaries and consequences, they are more likely to respect

A parent-child relationship where reasonable boundaries are established and enforced is the best environment for raising children who know how to avoid dangerous substances.

Substance Abuse Boundaries

Taking into account age-appropriateness for your children, you may want to consider adopting the following boundaries related to drug and alcohol use in your family.

- We will not allow any drinking, smoking, or illicit drugs in the house.
- When you want to attend your friend's party or sleepover, we must talk to the parents first and understand what supervisory arrangements are in place.
- We need to understand where you are going and who you are with and be comfortable with the behavior you will see modeled.
- As parents, we will administer prescription medications, rather than allowing children free access to them.
- As parents, we choose to apply a boundary to ourselves so that we can model the desired behavior to our children.
- We expect you to be responsible by committing to be home by the agreed-upon curfew.

whatever boundaries they are given regarding substance abuse?

A parent-child relationship where reasonable boundaries are established and enforced is the best environment for raising children who know how to avoid dangerous substances. But a key thing to remember here is that the boundaries have to be "reasonable." If they are not, they can be counterproductive.

The Drawbacks of Bad Boundary Setting

Parents can make mistakes with regard to boundaries at one extreme or another. I've known parents who have instituted far too few boundaries for their children. I've also known parents who have created too many boundaries, or too restrictive boundaries, for their kids. Both extremes are harmful. So we need to ask ourselves, what happens in the absence of boundaries or when they are too harsh?

While having reasonable boundaries helps children grow, having too few, too harsh, or inconsistent boundaries can be harmful to children. I can think of three important ways in which bad boundary setting can be harmful.

It can cause a child to feel insecure in his relationship with his parents. If a child always has to second-guess his parents, usually it's a sign of inconsistent parenting. This can cause the child to feel no small amount of anxiety, not knowing how Mom or Dad will react, and even be fearful of what may happen.

Young children, especially, tend to be concrete thinkers. You've got to tell them clearly what you expect of them and what will happen if they don't obey. Changing your mind by not following through on the delivery of a consequence one day, and yet being firm with its introduction on another day, is confusing and upsetting to a child.

It can cause a child to become bitter or resentful toward his parents. "You'll just have to learn the hard way!" Sound familiar? This is often referred to as the "school of hard knocks" syndrome. It is where parents fail to establish proper boundaries for their children, either because they don't perceive boundaries to be important or because they simply don't know how to go about it.

What is the result of this? Usually, it's a child who grows up to become bitter or resentful toward his parents. Although this child may have enjoyed his "freedom" at times during childhood, he realizes eventually that his parents didn't provide a safe environment for him to learn and grow in. If he learned anything, it was the hard way. He hurt himself, got hurt, or failed and only then discovered that he needed to do something differently to get a better result.

Harsh or unrealistic boundaries, then, can result in a child turning against his parents. Frustration, anger, disappointment, and hurt are always just around the corner.

It can send the wrong messages to the child about himself and his family. Depending on the type of failure in their boundary setting, parents can give a child different wrong and harmful ideas. Here are some of those messages:

- *I am never good enough.* This is where the child can never quite measure up to the expectations of one or both parents, no matter how good he is or how hard he tries.
- *I'm only loved if I do what my parents want.* In this situation a child begins to learn that the love of his parents is available to him only on certain conditions. He has to work hard to earn their love.

- *I must fear my parents to show them that I respect them.* In the presence of harsh or unrealistic boundaries and consequences being handed out by a parent, the child hears that the parent is to be obeyed and feared at all cost. This results not only in an environment of fear but also of mistrust. If the child oversteps the mark, then he is inclined to hide it for fear of retribution. From the other side of the fence, the parent begins to constantly question and become suspicious that his son is not behaving, sometimes resulting in the delivery of harsher penalties.

- *My parents are out of touch with my world.* Essentially, this is where the child feels as though the parent doesn't understand his world and that the parent is not interested in taking the time to appreciate his world. In the mind of the child, this creates a significant credibility issue. He sees such a huge contrast between how his mom and dad relate to him and how other parents (especially parents of his friends) relate to their children that he doesn't attach much value to what his mom and dad tell him.

Messages like these, and the other drawbacks of poor boundary setting, are depressing to consider. But thankfully, they make up only half the picture.

The Advantages of Good Boundary Setting

Don't let the possible effects of bad boundaries scare you away from setting boundaries and sticking with them. You are

fully capable of establishing good boundaries for
your kids and following
through on them. And
when you do so, you'll
experience the benefits in
your relationship with your
child.

> You are fully capable
> of establishing good
> boundaries for your kids
> and following through on
> them.

- Your child will be responsible for his emotions, attitudes, and behavior.
- Your child will feel more secure and confident.
- Your child will trust you and listen to you.
- Your child will have greater respect for himself and for others.
- Your child will learn how to make wise decisions.
- Your child will be kept safe from harm while gradually taking on independence.

And let's not forget what brought us all to *Talking Smack* in the first place. Although setting healthy boundaries will help your child in all areas of life, that most definitely includes the area of substance abuse. *The consistent use of all boundaries helps children stay within the particular boundaries related to drug and alcohol use.*

Look again at some of those words listed above in the advantages of good boundary setting. Secure. Confident. Responsible. Trusting. Respectful. Wise. Safe. A child with these qualities will be able to say no to drugs and alcohol when they are offered to him. A child with these qualities will be so busy pursuing a great future for himself that he will have little temptation to be sidetracked by substances that can do him no good.

I hope you will take the message of boundaries to heart. If you do, then when the time comes for your active parenting days to end (and believe it or not, that really will happen!), you will have the joy of knowing that you are setting an adult free into the world who is ready to establish a happy, healthy, and productive life for herself. After all is said and done, isn't that what you want?

That image of our child enjoying a happy adulthood is a beautiful picture. But before we get ahead of ourselves, we still have to consider guidelines for protecting our children from drugs and alcohol in the crucial teen years.

Chapter 5 Summary

Principles about setting healthy boundaries for your children:
- Parents should set reasonable boundaries, with appropriate consequences, for key areas of their children's behavior.
- While having reasonable boundaries helps children grow, having too few, too harsh, or inconsistent boundaries can be harmful to children.
- The consistent use of boundaries helps children stay within those particular boundaries that are related to drug and alcohol use.

FOR PARENTS OF OLDER CHILDREN

*How do I protect my middle schooler or
high schooler from drugs and alcohol?*

A ll of the guidelines covered in the preceding two chapters are just as relevant to teenagers as they are to younger children. With teens in the house, you still need to be talking about healthy living and modeling it, educating them about dangerous substances and the misuse of medication, and helping them to remember that violating your expectations for them will result in negative consequences. Most especially, you need to be establishing and enforcing boundaries to keep them safe.

But still, talking with an adolescent about drinking and drugs is a dramatically different matter compared to doing the same with a young child. The primary differences when your child reaches the teenage years are these:

- the ability to reason and discuss at deeper levels
- the desire for greater independence

- the tendency to engage in greater risk-taking activities and therefore face challenges (including the pressure to experiment with illegal substances) at a higher level of intensity

If you weren't convinced that drugs and drinking were issues you had to bring up with your child before he entered high school, I think you were wrong about that. But in any case, the situation has definitely changed now. Your teenager is at an age when you cannot avoid the subject. Not if you love your child. Whether it is in the classroom or from friends and acquaintances, your adolescent child is hearing about drugs and booze. For this reason alone, there is no need to apologize to your son or daughter for raising the subject.

> Your teenager is at an age when you cannot avoid the subject of drugs and alcohol. Not if you love your child.

But will you do it well? You can if you take into account the changes that come with your child's growing up. To help you in this, I've got a couple of additional guidelines for you to put in your memory bank. The first of them is one that did not come naturally to a dad named Tom.

Tom and Nicole

Tom was lying in bed, waiting for his fourteen-year-old daughter, Nicole, to return home from a friend's party. As he watched his digital clock tick past 11:00 p.m., he murmured to himself, "Curfew time. I just can't trust her." He threw back the blankets and headed downstairs to wait for what he hoped was Nicole's imminent arrival. Meanwhile, his wife, Tracy, knowing that a storm was brewing, thought it best to stay in bed.

Five minutes passed, then ten, then twenty, then fifty. Tom felt himself getting more and more angry. "This is unbelievable!" he said to himself.

Just as he said that, a key turned in the lock. Nicole entered.

Tom glared at Nicole and said in a raised voice, "I thought I could trust you. Clearly I was wrong!"

Nicole was about to respond but couldn't get a word out before Tom informed her that she was grounded for a month.

"You're always on my case!" Nicole screamed at her father. "You never leave me alone!"

To her, it was plain that her father couldn't accept the fact that she was not his little girl anymore. She had grown up.

She ran up the stairs and slammed her bedroom door shut.

Tom felt ready to explode. *How dare she yell at me when I'm trying to help her?* he thought. He started climbing the steps to continue the argument with his daughter. But suddenly he caught himself. *I need to calm down*, he said to himself. *Getting into a yelling match would only make matters worse.*

Wisely, he went to the kitchen to make himself a hot chocolate. He made another for Tracy when she came down in her dressing gown a few moments later.

"I'm at a loss as to what to do next," he said to his wife.

"I know," she replied. Tracy understood that Tom loved Nicole deeply and at the same time was very concerned about their teen's sudden need for independence. She sat down next to her husband and put her arm around him.

After a few moments of silence, Tom turned to Tracy and said, "I guess my role as a parent is changing, isn't it? I can't be there for her in every situation like I used to be when she was younger, and I struggle with that.

"However, I don't want to push her away, either," said Tom. "I think I'm trying to protect her from making the same mistakes I made when I was a teenager. I don't want to see her get hurt."

Tracy nodded her head reassuringly. Then she suggested to Tom an idea that she had been testing.

"When I think back to when I was the same age as Nicole," she said, "I remember that my parents appeared to take on more of a coaching role with me. The last couple of weeks, I've been trying to do the same with Nicole. She seems to be more responsive to me when I 'coach' her rather than 'tell' her."

"That's interesting," replied Tom. "I have noticed a change in your relationship with Nicole. You both seem closer than you were a couple of months ago, when you were banging heads together."

"Hey, I'm not the perfect coach," said Tracy, "but it sure beats collapsing into bed emotionally exhausted and wondering what I'm going to do differently the next morning."

She continued, "You should give it a try."

Tom nodded. "It can't get any worse, I guess!"

Tracy ruffled Tom's hair and said, "Come on, it's time to get some sleep. Things will look clearer in the light of day, and besides, I'm about to turn into a pumpkin!"

Tom agreed and followed Tracy up the stairs to bed, already thinking about how he would patch things up with Nicole the next day.

Coach Mom and Dad

Learning *what* to say to your teenage child and *when* to say something is a great gift to have as a parent. Unfortunately, it doesn't seem we are born with this gift. Like Tom, we have to learn that our role as parents will invariably change as our children grow and want to stretch their wings. While this desire for independence is perfectly normal, it is not without stress for the parent, who until now has been able to call the shots. (Okay, *most* of the time!)

You started off as your child's primary protector when she didn't have the ability to protect herself or understand the reasons behind the boundaries you set. Now she is beginning to question, argue, and dialogue with you about the values and principles you have raised her on. Although you don't lose the responsibility of protecting your daughter, it is no longer as easy to do this as it was when she expected you to. Now she feels as though she can handle some of the situations on her own—without you. This is a hard truth to swallow. But here's the thing to learn: it's time to *shift to a coaching role with your children.*

> We have to learn that our role as parents will invariably change as our children grow and want to stretch their wings.

So, what does it mean to be a coach instead?

Sometimes it means being willing to give advice from the sidelines and waiting for her to invite you into the game for one-to-one coaching. At other times it means painfully watching from a distance, disagreeing with a choice she has made but knowing she is going to need you to be there when things don't go the way she expected.

The easiest way to consider how to transition to becoming a coach your child can trust is to think about the role athletic coaches have played in your life. What caused some coaches to stand out more than others? How did they achieve the results they did?

More often that not, coaches coach because they want to. They are motivated to see people develop the skills necessary to perform well and ultimately to win games. They have a strong commitment to the sport and to the individuals who want to participate. They encourage players to work as a team and to respect each other and their opponents. They have a game plan. If something is not working or the team is not doing well, the coach tries another play or moves players around to compensate for weak areas. They are willing to experiment with different ideas. There are no shortcuts.

Similarly, parental "coaches" of teenagers need qualities like these:

- the ability to listen and empathize, sometimes avoiding the temptation to immediately correct
- organization and preparation, anticipating some of the challenges and thinking ahead so that they will know what to do and what options are available

- a high degree of patience and grace, knowing that many good things can be learned from failure
- the ability to create and provide an environment for healthy communication

Coaching is a skill every parent of a teenager needs to learn. But it's important to understand that shifting to a coaching role does not preclude talking directly and frankly with your child about the perils of drinking and taking drugs. That's something we still need to do—now more than ever.

Let's take a look at how to do that.

Tips for Talking to Your Teen

I'd be a wealthy man if I had a dollar for every time somebody asked me the question "How do I talk to my teenager about drugs?" The problem is, there is no one-size-fits-all answer to that question. How you talk to your teenager about drugs will depend on such things as these:

- the nature of your relationship with him
- how well the two of you communicate
- how well you respect each other
- whether he is used to having you provide input into his decisions
- how he handles pressure from his peers
- how confident you are in talking to him about drugs
- the presence of risk and protective factors in his life

So you need to spend some time assessing your relationship with your teen and planning an approach that works for you. Trust yourself. You know your child and you know yourself—you should be able to figure out some effective ways of discussing alcohol and drugs.

Having put the burden on you like that, however, I *can* offer you some practical tips to help you with your adolescent. These tips have proved to be generally true with most, if not all, middle and high school students. They boil down to this: *be bold and be caring.* Your child will appreciate it—eventually, anyway!

Stay involved in your teen's world. When teenagers express a desire for greater independence, many parents get the message and decide to accommodate the desire . . . to an extreme. Perhaps out of respect for their children, or perhaps because it's a convenient excuse for not doing anything, they disengage from their child's world. *Well, he's making up his own mind about things now*, they think.

This is a mistake and can be damaging to your child. Shifting to a coaching relationship is not the same thing as withdrawing. Your child still needs to be affirmed and loved, and he needs to know that home is a safe haven to which he can return even when he has made mistakes and has disappointed you. Keep paying attention to what is going on in your teen's life, and keep working with your teen to make wise decisions.

Get past the resistance. Your teen may be seeking your help or advice but is too proud or embarrassed to admit that he needs it. So listen not only with your ears but also with your eyes and your heart. Then look for creative ways to get a message to him that he needs to hear from you. Importantly, don't try to make every opportunity a time to say, "I told you so" or "If only you had listened." This is not a battle over who is right or wrong but instead an opportunity to ensure that he knows you care enough to give advice.

Be honest with your views. It's important that your child knows how you feel about him, about the friends he hangs out with, and about substance abuse. Look for opportunities to give positive (and genuine) input rather than merely express concerns. He may also want to know why you feel the way you do. It's not adequate to say, "Because that's just the way it is, okay?" Think through your rationale and how you might articulate it.

Give your child a network. When we hear someone mention peer pressure, we immediately think of it in a negative way. However, peer pressure can also be a positive influence in your child's life if you have helped him to know what characteristics to look for in a friend. Furthermore, finding one or more mentors for your child whom he can respect and receive feedback from as he journeys through the teenage years into adulthood can be a lifesaver. Look for ways to expand his network of support through relationships you have

> Peer pressure can be a positive influence in your child's life if you have helped him to know what characteristics to look for in a friend.

Conversation Starters to Use with Your Teen

As with younger children, you can use questions periodically to learn about your teen's world.

- "If there was one thing I could do for you today, what would that be?"
- "What is your biggest fear?"
- "Why do you think your friends text-message each other so much?
- "How do you cope with pressure from your peers to do things that you disagree with? What do you tell them?"
- "What things do you look for in a friend?"
- "Why is [insert name] your best friend?"
- "How would you describe yourself to someone who didn't know you?"
- "What activity do you enjoy doing the most with your family?"
- "What special talent or gift do you wish you had, and why?
- "What would make up the best weekend for you?"
- "Why do you think some of your friends experiment with drugs?"
- "Why do some of your friends go binge drinking on the weekend?"
- "If a friend asked you to go to a party where you thought there would be alcohol and drugs, how would you respond?"

> The important thing to remember in asking ques-
> tions like the ones above is that this is not a fishing
> expedition. It is a genuine desire to engage your teen-
> ager's world and understand it so that you can coach
> him along his journey.

developed at church, with other parents at school, or with neighbors.

Attack the issue, not your child. It is inevitable that your child will sometimes (or even frequently) disappoint you, deliberately or unintentionally hurt you, and place herself in situations where she is at risk. For you as a parent, it is only natural to want to jump in and do all you can to prevent that from happening. Unfortunately, if you believe that you are not being listened to or that your child has not taken your advice, you may feel the urge to attack your child with emotionally charged words that exacerbate the situation rather than focus on the issue. If you feel that you cannot successfully address the issue without getting angry or exasperated, then address it at another time when you feel more in control of your emotions. Or find someone your child respects and ask that person to help you.

These are just some of the practical tips that can help you in your conversation with your teen. And all of this becomes very real very fast when you are not just trying to prevent a problem but have a suspicion that your child is already experimenting with drink or drugs. After all, that's a strong possibility when a child has reached the teen years.

Chapter 6 Summary

Guidelines for protecting your middle schooler or high schooler from drugs and alcohol:

- Shift to a coaching role with your children.
- In talking with your teen, be bold and be caring.

INTERVENTION

What can I do if I suspect (or know) that my teen is already drinking or using drugs?

So far, we have looked at the importance of creating a strong parent-child relationship, working on effective communication, and being informed about drug and alcohol abuse and the potential consequences. However, as we read earlier in the book, you can be the best parent in the world and there will still be no guarantee that your teenager won't experiment with drugs, be tempted to smoke tobacco, abuse prescription medication, or go on a drinking binge with friends.

In fact, as much as we want to believe our children won't do these kinds of things, research tells us the opposite. In one recent national survey, we learned the following facts:[4]

- More than a third of twelve- to seventeen-year-olds (or 8.7 million) can get their hands on prescription drugs to get high within a day. And nearly one in five teens (4.7 million) can get them within an hour. Teens said prescription drugs were easier to buy than beer.

- Sixty-five percent of twelve- to seventeen-year-olds who drink get drunk at least once in a typical month. This increases by a further 20 percent for seventeen year olds.

- Compared to teens who have never tried alcohol, teens who get drunk monthly are eighteen times more likely to have tried marijuana, four times more likely to know someone their age who abuses prescription drugs, and more than twice as likely to know someone their age who uses meth, ecstasy, cocaine, heroin, or LSD.

One other startling revelation is that between 2007 and 2009, there was a 37 percent increase in the percentage of teens twelve- to seventeen-year-olds who indicated that marijuana was easier to buy than cigarettes, beer, or prescription drugs (19 to 26 percent).

If this makes you want to run away and put your head in the sand and pretend this will not happen to your teenager, then stand in line! It's perfectly normal to feel that way. But it's not going to help.

Signs of Drug and Alcohol Abuse

Before we look at what you can do if you suspect your teen is using drugs or drinking, it's important to know what to look for. What are some of the signs of substance abuse?

Signs of drug and alcohol use fall on a continuum ranging from subtle to not so subtle to obvious. As you will see, there is a progression of intensity and a move toward more overt behaviors that are not easily attributable to normal adolescent challenges.

The underlying message for you is this: *Be alert to signs of substance abuse in your child.* The following information will help you.

Subtle signs. Alert, caring parents can notice changes taking place in their children. Of course, changes are always taking place in teens—that's practically the definition of adolescence! But ask yourself if you have seen these changes in your teen:

- Secrecy
- Change in friends
- Change in dress and appearance
- Increased isolation
- Change in interests or activities
- Loss of interest in school, resulting in declining grades at school
- Inability to keep a job
- Changes in your child's personality and extreme changes in behavior at home
- Staying out all night and frequently exceeding curfew
- Regular use of eye drops to counter bloodshot eyes
- Sudden change in diet that includes cravings for sweets and junk food
- Dropping out of sports activities

I vividly recall going through this first list with a group of parents and having one of the dads interrupt the session by saying, "Most of these characteristics seem typical of most teenagers!" Clearly there was an element of truth in this, as it took a while for the laughter to subside. The key here is not to look for something negative or wrong behind every action or situation. There could be other things happening in your child's life that are causing this. The important thing is to be aware and vigilant.

> The key here is not to look for something negative or wrong behind every action or situation. It is to be aware and vigilant.

The frequent presence of these factors, particularly if there are more than two or three, should pique your interest.

Not-so-subtle signs. Moving on from symptoms that may be ambiguous indicators of substance abuse, we come to some similar kinds of symptoms—but ones that are more intense and more worrisome. Beware of these taking place in your teen's life:

- Extreme withdrawal from the family
- Depression
- Skipping classes or missing school on some days
- Mysterious telephone calls that produce frantic reactions
- Frequently waking up feeling sick, tired, or grumpy
- Financial problems
- Extreme weight loss or gain
- Appearance of new friends, who may be older than your child
- Rebellious and argumentative behavior

- Frequent lying about your teen's whereabouts, activities, or friends
- Long periods of time spent in the bathroom
- Acting disconnected, vague, forgetful, "spaced out," or having a shorter attention span than usual

The presence of any of these symptoms in your teen's life should give you concern. As with the more subtle signs, the cause might not be drug or alcohol abuse, but you're right to want to figure out exactly what is going on.

Obvious indicators. Finally we get to the third list of symptoms. And here you've got a real problem.

- Drug paraphernalia (such as vials, small bags, mirrors, pipes, tubes, razor blades, cigarette papers, foil, butane lighters, scales, matches, eye drop containers, cut-off hoses) found in the bedroom or hidden around the house
- Possession of large amounts of money
- Needle marks on the arms, sometimes deliberately hidden by clothing
- Money and valuables missing from the house
- Uncontrollable bursts of laughter with no apparent reason
- Dilated or pinpoint pupils
- Puffy or droopy eyelids
- Mention of suicide or an attempt at suicide
- Disappearance or dilution of bottles in the liquor cabinet or wet bar

- Time spent with people who you know use drugs or drink alcohol
- Medicine disappearing from the medicine cabinet
- Defense of friends' rights to use drugs or drink alcohol

While not comprehensive, the signs on this list convey a reality that every parent fears—that his or her teenager has a drug or alcohol problem that cannot be ignored. Typically, the presence of these factors indicate that your child is not merely experimenting or starting out but has been using for some time. Although some of the symptoms above may be evidence of other medical issues, one thing is absolutely clear: you cannot afford to let the symptoms mount or assume that your child is just going through a stage.

Very common for parents at this point of discovery is a desire to panic, become anxious, overreact, and get extremely angry with their children. Unfortunately, as normal and cathartic this might be, it is not healthy or constructive in seeking better outcomes for your child. The first thing to do at this point is to follow some simple rules of engagement in order to effectively intervene with a view to seeing a change in your teen's behavior and lifestyle.

Rules of Engagement

It is difficult for parents when they discover that their child is using drugs. Before jumping headfirst into addressing your concern with your teen, though, there are a few simple things you can do to prepare for the conversation that will need to take place between you and your teen. The key is to *think before acting.* You'll save yourself woe if you do.

Prepare yourself. Get yourself in hand before trying to deal with the problem you've uncovered in your teen. This has several aspects.

First, don't panic and don't overreact. The worst thing you can do right now is get angry at your child and lose control. You need to be as calm as you can be and try to understand why your child is taking drugs and how much of a problem it is.

Also, don't blame yourself. It is normal to feel that you have failed your child or begin telling yourself that you have been a lousy parent. But this is not a healthy time to focus your energy and emotions in a destructive way on your parenting.

And then, I advise that before you talk to your teen, you talk to others about a possible course of action. If you know of other parents who have shared a similar experience, learn from them. Certainly, don't be afraid of seeking professional help. It's also important to know what substance your child is taking and its effects so that you can be prepared in an emergency.

> If your child is using drugs or alcohol, it is normal to feel that you have failed your child or begin telling yourself that you have been a lousy parent. But this is not a healthy time to focus your energy and emotions in a destructive way on your parenting.

Finally, think about how the rest of the family is going to react. It's not unusual to neglect the needs of other family members when so much energy is focused on the child using drugs. Talk to the others honestly about what's happening. Affirm them and reassure them, because they are going to need you more than ever, and you are going to need them.

Create the right environment for talking to your child. Picking when, where, and how you will bring up the issue of drug or alcohol abuse with your teen is critical. It can make the difference between a conversation that leads to a turnaround in your teen's life and one that makes matters worse. Here is some helpful advice:

- Pick a place for the conversation where your child feels safe and comfortable.
- Decide on a time that would be best for you to get your teen's attention and cooperation.
- Seek to understand rather than jump down your child's throat. Plan to ask open-ended questions like "If you were me, how do you think you would feel about this?" and "How can I help you?"
- Don't fall for the trap of labeling your child because she has made a mistake or fallen short of your expectations. Saying "You're a failure . . . disappointment . . . good-for-nothing" will hurt rather than help.
- Figure out how to give feedback and empathize with your child. Whether your child admits it or

not, he needs to hear that you will not abandon
him and that you love him.

- Look for ways to stimulate change. You will
  want to ask your teen about the changes he
  would like to make and how would he like you
  to help. Remember, you're a coach!

Have a game plan. No football coach goes into a game
without a game plan or a set of plays to counter the other
team's strengths and weaknesses. Similarly, it is important to
try to anticipate how your child might respond. If things don't
go as you hope, what is your backup plan?

Although your child might be responsive to your sitting
down with her and wanting to help her, there is no guarantee
of that. Your child could get angry, defensive, not want to talk,
and even walk out without telling you where she is going.
However, by taking steps to prepare yourself first, creating the
right environment to talk to your child, and having a game
plan and backup plan, you are miles ahead of the parent who
chooses not to deal with the situation.

So, what does a game plan look like?

Again, there is no particular science or order of events that
will work every time. However, here are some things that are
more helpful than others, and the list below provides you with
some things to consider as you prepar a discussion with your
teen about drugs or drinking.

- Assess the situation. Understand why your child
  is using drugs or drinking alcohol.
- Consider what boundaries might need to be put
  in place to protect and support your child.

- Consider what boundaries might need to be put in place to protect and support the family.
- Ask a mentor, coach, teacher, or counselor whom your teen respects to talk to your child.
- Know what professional help is available to you and your child in your local area.
- Consider treatment options if your child has been using drugs for a substantial period of time.

One important thing to remember here is that until your teen has taken full responsibility for his actions, you must look at every day as an opportunity for intervention, no matter how small.

Problem-Solving Scenarios

To prepare for the unexpected, it is sometimes helpful to anticipate realistic scenarios and think through how you might respond if they were to happen. I have included three scenarios for you to consider. Take some time to sit down with your spouse to work out a game plan.

While it is likely that none of the three specific situations listed below will ever happen to you (I hope not!), it is still a valuable exercise to *prepare yourself for possible scenarios.* The examples below will help you get started with that.

Scenario 1

Your teen comes home from staying at his friend's place for the weekend, only for you to receive a telephone call from the friend's mom expressing concern that some money and other valuables have gone missing. You are doubly worried about this since you previously noticed money disappearing from your purse or wallet.

What's your game plan?

Scenario 2

You are asked to meet with the principal of your teen's school. When you do so, you learn that your daughter has been skipping classes and in some cases has been absent for an entire day. And beyond that, it turns out, yesterday your teen and three other students were discovered taking prescription drugs.

What's your game plan?

Scenario 3

As you are hanging up your child's laundered clothes in his closet, you smell something unusual and try and find out what it is. You stumble across a strange-looking implement with a tube coming out of it. When you talk to your child about this, he gets defensive and angry with you for entering his room.

What's your game plan?

Whatever specific challenge may come up in your family related to drugs or drink, you have to be prepared. You have

STEADY As You Go

The following six practical tips will help you restore or build a healthy relationship with your children. This creates a strong foundation when it comes to discussing tough issues with your kids, such as drug use. To help you remember the tips, I've used the acronym STEADY, reminding you that it requires steadfast commitment to engage your children on a difficult subject.

Seek forgiveness—As needed, ask your children to forgive you for past failures. (And be willing to forgive yourself as well.) I am amazed when I hear some parents equating apology with weakness, believing that to say you're sorry to your child merely allows the child to walk all over you. The opposite is true. When we ask forgiveness from a position of sincerity and humility, it is amazing how this "weakness" results in a stronger relationship where respect wins the day.

Time—Make up your mind that you won't use busyness as an excuse, and schedule time with your kids by putting a time for conversation in your calendar as a nonnegotiable appointment. Don't let your children tell you it's not important! Although modern-day technology has performed wonders in terms of providing efficient communication, it is amazing how this can overrun our family time. I have been reminded of this because my ten-year-old son has become sensitive about my checking my iPhone for e-mails and voicemails. The other day I overheard him saying to his mother, "Dad's on his iPhone again!"

Expectations—Be honest with your children about your fears, anxieties, and mistakes. Let them know what you are learning from them. This will give them confidence that you will love them even if they fail.

The ability to be clear with them also helps to prevent them from second-guessing what you expect from them. As my father used to say, "Confusion leads to chaos!"

Anger management—Introduce communication boundaries for your home. Your rules could include these: "We won't yell at each other. We won't criticize or put each other down. We won't call each other names."

The need for these boundaries is rooted in respect. When you can talk to me properly, I have a better chance of understanding.

Discuss—Negotiate with your family some realistic goals that can be achieved in the short term and write them down. A simple way to look at this is to ask each other, "What would you like to see, do, and be?"

> **Y**ou—Identify three things you wish you had received from your parents, and contemplate how you can go about giving these to your children.

to be practical. You have to act. Have faith in yourself—you can do it.

But I'm worried about something: maybe I've depressed you. Maybe you know that you have neglected to talk to your child for too long. Maybe your relationship with him has deteriorated to the point where you're not sure he'll listen to you if you try.

Is it too late for you to do any good?

Never Too Late

I can still vividly recall a late-night conversation I had with Terry, a fifty-four-year-old man who was lamenting the fact that he had made a mess of parenting his two sons and one daughter. All three had grown up, left home, and moved into different careers, but still the father blamed himself for having neglected them for much of their childhood as he traveled on business.

With tears welling up in his eyes, Terry whispered, "I failed them."

I shared with him that, while he could not change the past, it wasn't too late for him to repair his relationship with his kids and make things better for the future. He didn't believe me at first, but he said he would try.

Months later I talked to Terry again. This time he told me how he had sought and received the forgiveness of his children. He said he now was relishing his relationships with his children and loving being a grandfather.

I share this story in case you are questioning if it is too late for you. Your children are probably not grown up and out of the house, as were Terry's. But they may be getting older and perhaps are growing emotionally distant from you. You might have said the wrong thing, or said the right thing at the wrong time, only to see your child run in the opposite direction.

If this is your situation, I know that you may be feeling guilt, shame, or regret. You may be angry with yourself for not doing better and blaming yourself each time your children make a poor decision—about drugs and alcohol or anything else. You may be feeling helpless and resigned to your children slipping away from your influence and judgment.

Please do not lose hope. And *never give up!* It is never too late to be a positive influence in the life of your child.

As parents, we naturally wish we could go back in time and erase those occasions in our children's lives when they have been hurt, including experiencing the consequences of a poor decision. Of course we can't do that. But although it might be too late to prevent your child from getting hurt from a bad decision, that doesn't mean you can't be an effective parent from this moment forward.

You can be like Terry and start over, regardless of

> Although it might be too late to prevent your child from getting hurt from a bad decision, that doesn't mean you can't be an effective parent from this moment forward.

where your relationship with your children is at. You can start being a positive influence in their lives in regard to drugs and alcohol and other choices.

I know many parents of teenagers who would say the same to you. One of them is named Yvette, and you'll hear more about her in the next chapter.

Chapter 7 Summary

Guidelines for intervening when you suspect your child of using drugs or alcohol:

- Be alert to signs of substance abuse in your child.
- Think before acting.
- Prepare yourself for possible scenarios.
- Never give up!

PART 2

Interview with a Mother and Daughter

REALITY PREPARATION

"We truly want to help protect you."

Having got this far in the book, you have come to understand the importance of being an informed parent who doesn't wait until the last minute to prepare your children for the threat of drugs and alcohol. The questions and answers we've considered in the chapters up to this point have given you principles you can use in conversing with your own kids. You should be feeling more confident in your role. You've learned a lot!

Still, I would understand if there's a question in your mind—a question like this: What might it all look like in real life?

Well, I'm going to show you.

This chapter and the following two present in raw and real form the interview I conducted with a mother and her twenty-year-old daughter in relation to drugs and alcohol. The story that comes out reveals a family where the parents did their best, went through some rough times with their daughters, and in the end came through the child-rearing years with adult children who understand that drugs and alcohol can imperil their future.

Starting in this chapter, you will meet the mother (Yvette) and the daughter (Lauren). They tell us about what happened between them as well as with the father (Tommy) and Lauren's siblings (Lee and Buck). This chapter focuses on how Yvette and Tommy tried to prepare their children to face the world of drugs that, sadly, teenagers can no longer avoid. As you read it, think over what you can learn from it about preparing your own kids for the reality of drugs and alcohol.

In what follows, I've changed all the names to protect privacy. Everything else you'll read about Yvette and Lauren and their family is real.

This is their story.

The Influence of Family and Friends

GLENN: (To Lauren) Has your mum ever sat down with you to talk about drugs?

LAUREN: Kind of.

GLENN: How old were you?

LAUREN: I don't know. I can't really remember sitting down to talk about drugs. We did talk about it, though.

GLENN: But not formally—is that what you're saying?

YVETTE: Over time we've had many discussions. Not formally. We've never sat down and said, "Okay, as mother and daughter, let's talk about drugs." But we've talked about it off and on as it was relevant to the conversation we were having.

GLENN: So, Lauren, when do you first remember your mum or your dad talking to you about drugs?

LAUREN: I can't remember. It happened when we would talk about what we saw some of our friends doing and when we weren't sure how to react or what to do.

YVETTE: Think back to some of those situations. What would that conversation look like?

LAUREN: I would tell Mom something like "We saw so-and-so last night, and she wasn't in a good place, and she was smoking pot. I was offered some but said no." Mom would say, "Well, what did you say?" and I'd say, "There was some pressure to try it out, but I didn't want to." Mom would then talk about the importance of possible consequences, and we would go back and forth talking about that for a while.

YVETTE: We tend to do lots of role-playing to help us think through different responses.

GLENN: So, you felt quite confident talking about drugs and other issues with your mum?

LAUREN: Yes, I did.

GLENN: Would you feel just as comfortable talking about these issues with your dad?

LAUREN: Not as comfortable. Sometimes I wasn't sure how he would react, because he's very protective of me. I thought he would just freak out!

GLENN: So it's not because you don't trust him; you're just not sure if he could sit down and listen without getting upset about things?

LAUREN: Yeah. I can still talk about things with my dad, but it's just different. I'm not afraid. It's just a little more intense.

YVETTE: He has a different approach.

GLENN: So he cares for you.

LAUREN: Definitely.

GLENN: But he wouldn't necessarily get into a conversation about things you could do or say that would help you address some of the challenging situations you face?

LAUREN: That's right.

GLENN: What about your sister? Did you feel comfortable talking about drugs and some of the issues you were likely to encounter in high school with her?

LAUREN: Yeah, most of the time. Usually, when we were at a friend's house or at a party with others from school, we would tell each other what was happening or what we saw.

GLENN: So it was a support to you having Lee [the sister] with you. How?

LAUREN: Yeah. We both know that drugs are one of those things that neither one of us is going to do.

GLENN: Why not?

LAUREN: I don't know. I'm not interested in it. I don't know what Lee would say, but I like to brag and say that I've never tried it. I've not tried anything. Drugs.

GLENN: What about cigarettes and alcohol?

LAUREN: Oh yeah.

GLENN: Is that because mum and dad have done a good job raising you, or . . .

LAUREN: Probably. (Laughter)

YVETTE: I ask my girls the same questions. I say, "Things like cutting, sex, drugs— have you tried these?" And they say, "We just don't; we're not there." But I say, "Why? I'm just curious. Why not?"

> I ask my girls the same questions. I say, "Things like cutting, sex, drugs—have you tried these?"

GLENN: Is it also because of the type of friends you have?

LAUREN: Sure.

YVETTE: Well, out of your group of friends, you guys are the only ones at this stage of your lives not into drugs.

GLENN: So it's not that you have good friends who feel the same way as much as you've seen the negative impact of some of their decisions on themselves, and you say to yourself, "That's not for me"?

LAUREN: That's certainly the case with some friends. There are times when it's not so much who you are with but what they might do. You have no idea sometimes that things are about to go in a different direction.

Parental Involvement

GLENN: (To Yvette) Listening to this, have you ever sat down with Tommy [the father] and said something like "Drugs are obviously going to be an issue for our kids, and our kids are going to have to be able to deal with it." How have you handled this? Have you and Tommy had a conversation about it?

YVETTE: Once again, probably not formally, and not specifically on the topic of drugs. What we have sat down and discussed, however, are things like the mistakes that we've made in the past prior to becoming Christians.

We've discussed, at what point do we sit down with the kids and talk about these things? And we've determined that there may be a day when that is necessary, or it may not be. What we have shared with our kids is that we have made mistakes. We've made plenty of mistakes. And so our parenting is coming out of trying to help steer our kids away from the same mistakes that our friends and we made. Mistakes that we can't go back and correct. Someday we'll sit down and talk about that.

> Our parenting is coming out of trying to help steer our kids away from the same mistakes that our friends and we made. Mistakes that we can't go back and correct.

GLENN: Yvette, some parents would say you should let your kids learn the hard way, perhaps the same way you did. Do you agree with that principle?

YVETTE: No. No. No. No. No way.

Lauren, how would you respond?

LAUREN: I know kids who do heaps of stuff and their parents just have no idea. I also think some of them would have given anything to have their parents be more interested in them and intentional about helping them make better choices. They don't see their parents caring for them.

GLENN: Is that what has meant the most to you, that your parents have cared enough to stay involved in your life?

LAUREN: Probably. Enough that they don't want to see me get hurt. The hard lessons are still there anyway. I see enough to understand the consequences of decisions others make and that I had the same choice.

The Parents' Privacy

GLENN: Yvette, while you and Tommy have never had a formal discussion about what to say to your kids about drugs, you described a turning point for both you and Tommy when you made a conscious decision to turn your back on a lifestyle characterized by lots of mistakes. How much of a motivation is this to you in trying to steer your kids in a healthy direction and see that the decisions they make today may have long-lasting implications?

YVETTE: We say that a lot. We talk to all three kids about the choices they make, and that the choices they make are *their* choices. As parents, our role is to help guide you through those choices, and teach you about consequences on the other side of them. There will be a day when we're not there to guide you, when we're not there 24/7. We know that there will be a day when you will understand, and that as you get older, the decisions you make have bigger and bigger consequences. So we've always talked about choices having consequences.

Lauren, would you agree?

LAUREN: Absolutely.

YVETTE: But that comes up in every area, whether it's financial or something else. You might have some pocket money, even as a kid, and you want to buy a toy or something. Next week you might be going to camp and don't have enough money saved. The choice you made to buy a toy has consequences. Anyway, I think as parents we've tried to apply choice and consequence in so much of what we've done and said along the way.

GLENN: Given that you and Tommy have taken the position that your past is irrelevant in that you don't have to talk about it with your kids, was there ever a time when you dreaded that your kids might ask you about your past? Did that possibility ever create some awkwardness or fear for you, or perhaps even that they may choose to listen to somebody else?

YVETTE: Yes, from the standpoint that when they get older they start realizing that their parents weren't perfect. When kids are younger, often their parents do seem perfect and that they never make mistakes. For Tommy and me, there has been that fear that when our kids start putting things together and realize we weren't perfect, they'll start asking questions about our past that we won't know quite how to respond. Out of our three kids, only one so far, has ever point-blank asked me direct questions, and that is Lauren.

GLENN: Lauren, was there any particular reason why you wanted to ask your mum those direct questions?

LAUREN: I don't know, really.

GLENN: Were you surprised at your mum's response?

YVETTE: Do you remember how I responded?

LAUREN: Yeah. You said that when I was old enough, and that today was not the day.

YVETTE: So, to answer your question, yes, you fear there are some days when they'll ask. And yet on the flip side, I could honestly say, "Not yet. We're not just there yet."

LAUREN: Although I'm still curious, it's reassuring to know that they were human, that they've been through something we haven't yet.

YVETTE: I think that is a big factor in the communication. We have always said, "We're not perfect, guys, and your dad and I would both tell you that we've made so many mistakes along the way. We truly want to help protect you from those mistakes as best we can. And yet your choices are going to have consequences." We've said that from when the kids were young.

Parenting with Authenticity

GLENN: It's interesting that you have been very honest with your kids, telling them that you've made some bad decisions in the past, and that a turning point in your life occurred when you and Tommy became Christians, resulting in a significant lifestyle change. I know many Christian parents who would find this honesty very difficult. Why do you think Christian parents, particularly, find it difficult to talk to their children about drugs?

YVETTE: I think as Christians we tend to put on our masks of who we are now, forgetting the past and moving forward, and the old is the old and the new is the new. Unfortunately, with that, we never let that mask down to be able to reveal truly the grace of God and how those who have been forgiven much, forgive much.

I tell my kids all the time I am the poster child for grace. I understand that parents don't want to relive the past by bringing it up with their kids. But sadly, it doesn't give credit to how much Jesus Christ loves us now—in spite of us. It's easier to say we just never want to talk about that again.

GLENN: The word "authentic" comes to mind here. It appears to me that you are saying there is a great need today for authentic parents who are willing to be transparent with their children about the challenges they once faced to demonstrate grace, forgiveness, and hope. Does that capture what I heard you say?

YVETTE: Yes. However, I think parents do need to be careful about the degree of detail they may feel pressured to give their children about past mistakes. The Bible references the need for people to not cause others to stumble. Sometimes it's the details that can lead to your children stumbling. For example, in relation to sexual sin and issues of promiscuity, lust, and impurity, there is no need to go into graphic details that may cause them to visualize all of the details that potentially may lead them to stumble unnecessarily. What I want my kids to know is, I have never been perfect, I will continue to make mistakes; but I also have a greater strength and wisdom to guide me through some of those imperfect moments when a choice I make can result in hurt or good.

The fear for parents is, while they have made mistakes and lived to tell the story, their children have yet to make some of those mistakes, and there is no guarantee that they will go through unharmed. Tommy and I tell our children, "When we made some of our mistakes, we were without Christ. You are with

Christ, and that makes such a huge difference in how you weigh your decisions and the choices you make."

GLENN: It is evident that some parents, particularly Christian parents, struggle in engaging their kids on the issue of drugs. One of the reasons for this is that they are unsure as to what to say or how to approach the topic, and if they do say something to their children, it might not be up to scratch. This creates a situation where there is the tendency to let the kids manage on their own and hope that they will get through this phase in life. In other words, because the parents fear failure, they run the risk of their children failing and making choices with some significant consequences.

YVETTE: Absolutely.

Lee and Lauren have just recently moved out, and we said to them, "When life hits you hard, and when you fail at things—not *if* life hits you hard, and not *if* you fail at things, but *when*—we are absolutely here for you both." The description we have given is, you have a security blanket under you when you fall, and you can do that here—whether it's good, bad, ugly, or different. That's our family dynamics. But I think you're exactly right. The parents of many of Lee and Lauren's friends are pretty rigid on these types of conversations and

> We said to them, "When life hits you hard, and when you fail at things—not *if* life hits you hard, and not *if* you fail at things, but *when*—we are absolutely here for you both."

afraid of what a discussion on drugs might lead their children to do.

The Talk among Friends

GLENN: Lauren, we've heard that many parents are fearful of raising the subject of drugs with their kids. What sort of discussions do you have with your friends? And do you see that you have a specific role in that?

LAUREN: There's one friend I have where her parents know that she's doing it [drugs]. When she was younger, she would ask me and her friends to help cover for her and even keep a change of clothes for her so she could change out of her clothes so that her parents couldn't smell pot on her. I would get so mad at her.

GLENN: What did you say?

LAUREN: I tried telling her that some of the people she would smoke with she didn't know well and that anything could go wrong. I've seen all sorts of things happen.

GLENN: What made you mad?

LAUREN: More the fact that she had all the intentions of doing stuff that wasn't good for her, and she is so much better than that. I told her that I would go with her to some places if that would help her to not do it.

GLENN: Do you think she felt pressure to smoke pot?

LAUREN: She has no self-esteem. I know that's a horrible thing to say, but it's true.

YVETTE: In the discussions that Lauren and I have had talking about friends and what kind of pressures you're facing, we've talked very openly about things—sex, drugs, and really anything. I always ask, "What do you think is driving that?" Typically, low self-esteem always comes up.

GLENN: By self-esteem, you mean how someone feels about herself in the context of her personal world, including how she thinks others see her and how good she is at some things?

LAUREN: Yes.

YVETTE: Lauren has a friend who has a severe eating disorder, a friend with cutting issues, and a friend that is really into drugs right now.

LAUREN: Yeah, she turned up at our apartment just the other night. She and two of her friends turned up totally stoned.

GLENN: So, what did you do?

LAUREN: We turned her away. She knows how Lee and I feel about that. She was doing well for a while and we were there for her. But right now she's being pretty stupid.

GLENN: Lauren, on a scale of one to ten, do you think Mom and Dad equipped you well to deal with some of the challenges you faced in high school?

LAUREN: I'd say a nine.

GLENN: Nine?

LAUREN: I'd say no one could be a ten. I think that's impossible.

Conclusion

So far in this interview with Yvette and Lauren, we have focused on the importance of a parent preparing her daughter to face some significant pressures—in this instance, drugs. All of this, in addition to showing us one family's journey, suggests helpful truths that we can use in our own family situations.

There's a lot more of Yvette and Lauren's story still to come! In the next chapter, we're going to see how their world was rocked.

Chapter 8 Summary

Principles from Yvette and Lauren about preparing children to face the threat of drugs and alcohol:

- A strong parent-child relationship can make all the difference in ensuring that a child will pay attention to warnings about drugs.
- Role-playing situations your child will likely encounter is one way to help her know ahead of time how to respond.
- Positive peer support (like Lee got from Lauren) can reinforce what the parents are teaching.
- Parents need discernment in knowing what information to share relative to their children's age and maturity.
- Parents can capitalize on teachable moments to reinforce the relationship between choices and consequences.
- Authentic parenting demonstrated in open, honest communication enables effective dialogue and questioning.

THE LEARNING INCIDENT

"I think I'm going to die!"

As we saw in the last chapter, Yvette and Tommy worked hard to prepare their children for the reality of substance abuse. Lauren even gave her parents a nine out of ten for their efforts in this area. (May all of our children be able to say the same!)

But this didn't guarantee that the children in the family would never give in to the allure of drugs or alcohol. As we'll soon learn, Lauren made the choice that many teenagers make—to experiment with a mood-altering substance. The way it turned out, the reality of what she experienced reinforced what her parents had been teaching all along. But it was a scary and unpleasant way to learn a lesson. Fortunately, not every parent has to hear the words "I think I'm going to die!" from a child, as Yvette heard from hers.

In this exchange we learn how Yvette and Lauren confronted one of those moments of truth that comes when children are growing up. I wonder how you and I would have handled the situation.

Exposure to Drugs

GLENN: (To Lauren) How old were you when you were exposed to drugs for the first time?

YVETTE: Can I ask a clarifying question? "Drugs." Do you mean alcohol and cigarettes as well?

GLENN: I'm assuming that the majority of kids today are exposed to alcohol and cigarettes from a young age, although there comes a time when they experience pressure to drink alcohol or smoke outside of the legal age. I'm really talking about illegal drugs such as marijuana, ecstasy, speed, meth, et cetera.

How old were you when you were exposed to these illegal drugs for the first time?

LAUREN: I never saw pot, or smelled it, or was ever around pot, until my sophomore year. I was sixteen years old.

GLENN: Okay. So while you were not directly exposed to drugs, were you aware of your friends being exposed to drugs or using them?

LAUREN: To a degree.

YVETTE: What about the boy who lived down the street from us? He would come down and say to you that he'd been smoking weed. You were only about eleven or twelve.

LAUREN: Oh yeah. But I don't think it quite clicked. Like, I think it was sixth grade when I first started hearing things about drugs outside of home and that they were supposed to be so bad for us. But it never occurred to me that, like, wow, he's doing drugs or smoking something that's really bad for him.

GLENN: So generally, your exposure was limited to smoking cigarettes, although pot as well, but at the time you didn't understand the difference?

LAUREN: Not really.

GLENN: What about alcohol? Binge drinking has been a growing phenomenon. Had you seen this?

LAUREN: No. Not until high school. Sixteen years old.

GLENN: How prevalent was it when you got to high school?

YVETTE: Extremely.

LAUREN: The first time I was exposed to something like this was when a couple of kids I knew came to school with Vicodin. They were completely doped up on V [Vicodin]. They were acting out pretty badly. So I think that was probably my first time.

Actually, there were a couple of kids in eighth grade who I remember always got in trouble. One of them died a couple of months ago from an overdose of meth and something else. When I heard about that, it was like, "Wow."

GLENN: This person was a friend?

LAUREN: No, more of an acquaintance that I knew from eighth grade. My sister knew him better. But he developed a pretty bad reputation.

The Party

GLENN: Let me change the subject a little here and dig into what can be described as a learning incident for you this year. Describe for me the lead-up to that experience.

LAUREN: We had no intention of it. We just went out to Red Robin to eat as friends. We're all sitting there, and we're like, "What shall we do?" One of the guys we were with had a water bottle filled with vodka that he was just sipping on. And one of the friends I invited said that he had a friend's place that was right behind where we were and that we could go there and watch a movie, listen to music, or whatever. Then one of the guys we were with said, "Let's stop and get some drinks for us." Of course, we all said, "No, no," before eventually saying, "Well, sure."

> One of the guys we were with said, "Let's stop and get some drinks for us." Of course, we all said, "No, no," before eventually saying, "Well, sure."

GLENN: So, this guy was older than twenty-one?

LAUREN: Yes.

GLENN: So you picked up some drinks.

LAUREN: Right.

GLENN: You went to the apartment.

LAUREN: Came back to the apartment, and then it was like, "I wonder what it would be like to get drunk?"

GLENN: Was Lee there?

LAUREN: Yeah.

GLENN: Do you know how Lee was feeling?

LAUREN: Unfortunately for her and her boyfriend, they were like, "Why don't you drink tonight? We've got your back, you have a ride home, and we're with friends."

GLENN: Were you curious? What was going through your mind? Was it simply "It would be nice to have a couple of drinks"? Or was it "This might be the night to get drunk and see what it feels like"?

> It was my intention at that point to get drunk, because I wanted to know what I would be like.

LAUREN: It was my intention at that point to get drunk, because I wanted to know what I would be like. You know, everyone turns into someone different when they're drunk—quiet, mean, crazy, you know.

GLENN: Because you've seen that?

LAUREN: Yeah. I wanted to know what I would be like. And there were a couple of people I wanted to get back at, I guess. I was often the DD—the designated driver.

GLENN: And those people were with you on that night?

LAUREN: No.

GLENN: So, how was this getting back?

LAUREN: I wanted to get drunk and call them to harass them. I always get these calls from some people when they're drunk into the night, and I thought, *It's my turn to do the same thing to them.*

GLENN: So you wondered what you were going to be like when you were drunk. At what point did you think you were going to be drunk, and how did you think you were going to know when you were drunk?

LAUREN: In hindsight, it was stupid, because I didn't know my limits. I'm only 130-plus pounds.

GLENN: How many drinks did you have?

LAUREN: Seventeen shots of terrible vodka that will (a) make you sick and (b) get you drunk that much faster.

GLENN: And were you sick?

LAUREN: I threw up all over myself. Earlier in the night, I had said to the guy whose house it was, "I don't know what I'm doing." And he said, "Just knock shots with me, because I get drunk pretty fast. So when I go drunk, then we'll stop." And I was like, "Okay."

GLENN: And did he stop?

LAUREN: He stopped after seventeen. And we did it so fast!

GLENN: You did seventeen straight. Did you have any chasers after some of them?

LAUREN: A couple of times. I had to have something to chase it down with, so I began mixing vodka and Coke. Which was horrible!

GLENN: So let me reflect on something here. Your friend said to you that he got drunk very quickly, so he obviously would've been drunk before he got to seventeen shots?

LAUREN: Right.

GLENN: So, who was watching out for the both of you?

LAUREN: Everyone else at the party.

GLENN: Where was Lee in this picture?

LAUREN: She was watching everyone else.

GLENN: She couldn't see you getting drunk?

LAUREN: Oh yeah, she could.

GLENN: And she felt . . .

LAUREN: She felt real bad afterwards.

GLENN: At other times during the night she probably thought you were okay?

LAUREN: Yeah. She was also watching her boyfriend, who was drinking.

GLENN: So pretty much it was all fun until when?

LAUREN: Until we stopped drinking shots.

GLENN: Why did you stop at seventeen?

LAUREN: We had used up all of the vodka.

GLENN: Had you started feeling ill yet?

LAUREN: No, that didn't hit until later, but I did start feeling a little crazy.

GLENN: You were mindful of that? You were conscious that you were feeling a little crazy, a little silly?

LAUREN: Right, but after a certain time, honest to God, I do not remember anything after that. I don't remember getting home.

GLENN: How did you get home?

LAUREN: Apparently Josh, the twenty-one year old, carried me on his back from the car to my house.

At Home

GLENN: Yvette, were you home?

YVETTE: Yes. We have a family rule that they have to come and let us know that they're home. We knew what time they had to be home, because they had a curfew. We later discovered that Lauren had been drinking for about the last hour and a half.

LAUREN: I started drinking around 10:30 p.m., and we were done around 12:30 a.m. because we had to be home at 1:00.

GLENN: What were the events that transpired once they got home?

YVETTE: Well, I was completely asleep. Lee checks in, and then they go out, and I go back to sleep. Then about twenty to thirty minutes later, Lee came back in to wake me up, and she said, "Mom, Lauren is upstairs and is really sick, and I need you to get up."

GLENN: Lauren, you were really sick at this point and vomiting?

LAUREN: I kind of remember getting home. I fell. Lee had to carry me to Mom's room. I was propped up on her, saying goodnight to Mom and Dad. I don't remember how I got upstairs. I do remember crawling into the bathroom, and then I threw up everywhere. I don't really remember much after that.

GLENN: So, Yvette, Lee has just come and woken you up.

YVETTE: Yes. It's about 1:20 a.m.

GLENN: And you've just heard "Mom, I need you. Lauren's really sick and I need your help."

LAUREN: I do remember having a conversation with my sister, although there are bits and pieces I can't remember. I was saying things like "I think I'm going to die!" And she would say, "No, I just think you're really drunk." Then I would say, "No, seriously, I need help right now!" Lee then said something like "If I go and get Mom, she's going to know that you're drunk and we're both going to be in trouble. Do you realize that?" I said, "I don't really care. I really need you to go and get Mom, because I am not okay. I don't care if we get in trouble."

GLENN: Lee was obviously concerned about getting into trouble.

LAUREN: Lee felt absolutely horrible. When she saw how sick I was, she just felt terrible.

GLENN: Was this your first binge-drinking incident?

LAUREN: Honestly, I've tried a couple of drinks at parties but never drank too much or been drunk before.

GLENN: Yvette, let's come back to you. Lee came and got you. What happened next?

YVETTE: I go upstairs. The week prior to this, Tommy had been sick with the flu, and I'm thinking, *My goodness, I hope she doesn't have what her dad had, because it was just horrible.* I get upstairs and she is lying on the floor with no clothes on, wrapped up in a blanket, and there is vomit everywhere. Everywhere! I said to Lee, "What is going on?" Lauren is crying and sobbing.

LAUREN: Because I also knew I had to tell her. I couldn't hide it.

YVETTE: She was crying, "Take me to the hospital. Take me to the hospital."

LAUREN: I didn't think I was going to make it. I really didn't. I was just feeling that sick.

YVETTE: So, she's crying, "Take me to the hospital," and I'm like, "What is going on?" And Lee said, "Mom, Lauren's been drinking." Then I said, "*What* has she been drinking, and *how much* has she been drinking?" Lee told me what Lauren had been drinking, but at that point she said, "I really don't know how much Lauren's been drinking."

GLENN: Yvette, what was going through your mind at this time?

YVETTE: You mean when she said that she had been drinking?

GLENN: Yes.

YVETTE: Probably my first response was *Okay, that explains a lot of what I was obviously seeing.* Then, Lauren crying and crying to be taken to hospital, I said, "No, Lauren, you're not going to the hospital. You're going to have to deal with this. That was the attitude of "Okay, little girl, this is what getting drunk is really like. There are consequences to your choices, and this is going to play out."[5]

> "Okay, little girl, this is what getting drunk is really like. There are consequences to your choices, and this is going to play out."

Then Lauren said, "But I think I'm going to die and I feel so sick." I replied, "These are all absolutely the things that go with drinking and being drunk. It's normal. It's going to have to wear off." I then reassured her that I would stay with her during that time. I went and got a cold rag, some ice chips, and said, "Honey, at this point you're not going to die, and you're not going to a hospital. It's going to wear off, and it's going to be a rough, hard road. But I'm not going to leave you. I'm going to sit here with you." I sat there, and Lee started filling me in on the story. We were there till 4:10 in the morning.

LAUREN: I was just crying, crying, and crying, saying over and over again, "I'm sorry, I'm sorry."

GLENN: Where was Lee at this point?

YVETTE: Sitting there with us. Three of us on the bathroom floor.

GLENN: Where was Tommy?

YVETTE: Sleeping.

GLENN: He didn't wake up?

YVETTE: He finally did, midstream of all of this, and said, "What's going on?" At that point Lee and I just looked at each other. What do we say? How much do we say? In my mind it was like, there is truth and then there is truth. This was definitely a moment of truth!

GLENN: What did you say?

YVETTE: Simply, Lauren's been drinking. I told him she had been drinking shots of vodka and that I didn't know how many. "She's very sick. I'm watching her. I'll stay with her and we'll deal with this tomorrow." At that point I said to Lee, "Why don't you go to bed? You get some sleep. I'll stay with her." It was about 3:00 a.m.

GLENN: How did Tommy react?

YVETTE: At one point Lauren was crying, saying, "Daddy, I don't drink." Tommy said, "Lauren, that may have been true earlier, but it's not true right now." Lauren continued crying, saying, "Daddy, take me to the hospital." He said, "No. You're just going to have to wear it off." He then went back to bed. Then, finally,

> At one point Lauren was crying, saying, "Daddy, I don't drink." Tommy said, "Lauren, that may have been true earlier, but it's not true right now."

about 4:10 in the morning, Lauren had calmed down and was starting to breathe and sleep and stopped vomiting. I got her pillow, cleaned up around her, and she stayed there. I went back to bed.

This was Thursday night, so I had a Friday and had to be work. I got up at 6:00 a.m. and checked on Lauren before waking her up at 7:00 a.m., because she also had to be at work at 10:00 a.m.

GLENN: Lauren, did you go?

LAUREN: Oh yeah.

YVETTE: I told her not to even think about calling into work sick. This was part of the consequences. "You will get up. You will shower. You will clean up this bathroom. You will go to work. And then we will be discussing this tonight."

LAUREN: To make things worse, I had to work a double shift that day.

The Feelings Afterward

GLENN: Let's fast-forward a little. Yvette, obviously you were disappointed.

YVETTE: Yes. Hurt and disappointed.

GLENN: Help me understand that more. Why did you feel hurt?

YVETTE: Hurt because we had always had such a great relationship and had such great communication. Also hurt because, if they hadn't got caught, if it didn't rise up to the extreme situation it did, I thought, *What else have you done that you haven't told me or got caught for? What else is there that you're not telling you me and your dad, and what else is there that is now hidden that needs to be brought out?*

GLENN: Are you talking about a form of betrayal?

YVETTE: Completely.

GLENN: So you felt that you had invested so much into Lauren, and that you had an honest, transparent relationship that you could talk about almost anything, and then this?

YVETTE: That's right. That's what hurt. Betrayal. Then came the disappointment. I said, "Lauren, my goodness, you know better. You understand consequences."

GLENN: Lauren, although you understood consequences and have experienced them before in relation to other things, did you ever think that the consequences for something like this would be so bad?

LAUREN: No. No idea.

GLENN: Looking back, I'm sure you have more of an appreciation for how people end up doing some really silly things when they're drunk that they later regret, because sometimes they don't remember. They can't recall what might have happened or didn't happen. It's like a total loss of control.

LAUREN: That's right. That scared me. I've been there.

GLENN: Yvette?

YVETTE: While I was hurt and disappointed, I was also re-lieved to God, because truly Lauren did experience alcohol poisoning. There was so much alcohol in her system, and I knew what could have happened. I just gave thanks to God that she was okay and that we made it through that hump.

Conclusion

Fortunately, Lauren didn't die, although she certainly went through a traumatic experience. And as for Yvette, despite being hurt and disappointed by Lauren's behavior, she remarkably sat with her in the darkness of the night and the moment.

Sadly, I have come across many parents who have faced similar situations but who have responded with "Oh, you poor baby! How were you to know what would happen?" End of story. No consequences. No lessons learned.

In the next chapter, Lauren wasn't so "lucky"!

Chapter 9 Summary

Principles from Yvette and Lauren about helping children through a crisis with drugs or alcohol:

- Parents can have the best relationship with their child, but there is no guarantee that the child will always make the best decisions.
- The wrong kind of friends can lead otherwise careful kids to make bad choices.
- Emotions like curiosity, boredom, anger, frustra-tion, and a desire for revenge can negatively influence a child's decisions.

- When a child loses control of her senses and her ability to think clearly, no matter where she might be, it puts her at considerable risk.
- When possible, parents may choose to let the natural consequences of a bad decision play out in a safe environment.
- It's better not to react to a bad decision immediately out of one's tiredness, disappointment, or hurt but rather wait to figure out what to do about it in the light of a new day.

FACING THE CONSEQUENCES

"What are we going to do with this?"

In a moment of curiosity and foolishness, Lauren decided to see what it was like to get drunk. The sickness that followed was enough to show her that it was a bad idea. But this didn't mean her parents were off the hook for responding.

At first Yvette and Tommy were dealing with some understandable emotions—surprise, shock, disappointment, hurt, fear. But then they got some moments to themselves to reflect on what had happened. They looked at each other, took a deep breath, and let out a long, drawn-out "Phew!" Finally there came those two infamous words: "Now what?"

> They looked at each other, took a deep breath, and let out a long, drawn-out "Phew!" Finally there came those two infamous words: "Now what?"

This was the first encounter like this they'd had as parents. They were feeling uncertainty. But they also had a steely determination to help Lee and Lauren learn a lesson from this experience that they would never forget.

Here is how my interview with Yvette and Lauren concluded:

Getting Ready to React

GLENN: Yvette, as a mother, what did you decide to do? How were you going to handle this? Had you given this much thought and determined toward a course of action for yourself, or did you discuss this with Tommy before Lauren arrived home?

YVETTE: Yes, we did discuss this.

LAUREN: Actually, I remember Mom and Dad asking us, "What do you want us to do? We've never done this before."

YVETTE: You've got to remember that this happened on Thursday night. Lauren worked her double shift. I had to go to work. We had something planned on Saturday. And so we determined as a family—including our youngest son, Buck—that we would all sit down and discuss this on Sunday morning.

Privately, Tommy and I said to each other, "What are we going to do with this?" To be honest, we just didn't quite know how it was going to play out, but we knew there had to be consequences.

GLENN: It was great that the two of you could openly discuss this with each other.

YVETTE: Absolutely.

GLENN: Some parents would find this very difficult.

LAUREN: I know parents who could never do what Mom and Dad did.

YVETTE: Tommy and I privately had to discuss this—"What would we do? What was appropriate? Where would we do it? What was our game plan?"—before speaking to the kids.

Cars and Consequences

GLENN: What did you decide to do? You sat down together for breakfast as a family. Was Buck there?

YVETTE: Yes. Actually, it was fun. Buck kept saying, "Okay, let me just do a note to self. I need a legal pad." He was taking down notes, watching, and learning.

GLENN: Lauren, at this point, you knew you weren't going to be caught off guard. You knew what the conversation was going to be about that morning. Were you nervous or anxious?

> Lee and I were thinking, *This is it. We're not going to have any life after this morning.*

LAUREN: Lee and I were thinking, *Our lives are over. This is it. We're not going to have any life after this morning.*

YVETTE: (To Lauren) What did transpire?

LAUREN: Well, we got another car out of the whole thing.

GLENN: You what? You got a new car? That's a consequence?

LAUREN: Well, not a new car, but another car. Mom and Dad said to Lee and me (because we shared the Ford Explorer), "Buck gets the truck, and we bought you our neighbor's VW Jetta."

GLENN: Hang on a minute. I don't understand how you jumped to "we got another car." How did the morning start?

YVETTE: We went out for breakfast.

GLENN: So you chose a safe place where you knew nobody could overreact and get angry?

YVETTE: (Laughter) Right.

LAUREN: Actually, that's exactly what I thought. It was like, *Thank God, we're going somewhere where there're other people!*

GLENN: Okay, so you've ordered breakfast. Who starts the conversation?

LAUREN: Dad.

GLENN: What did Dad say?

YVETTE: He said, "Tell us what happened."

LAUREN: More like, "Basically, what's wrong with you?"

YVETTE: "What were you thinking? What was going through your mind?"

GLENN: Then what?

YVETTE: Tommy led the conversation pretty much at this point, talking about the consequences of this. "You've lost our trust. That is going to have to be earned back."

LAUREN: Which for Lee and me was the biggest consequence, over taking any material thing away from us. It was the fact that we hurt them and lost all of our trust. That was the biggest consequence for us.

> "You've lost our trust. That is going to have to be earned back."

YVETTE: The biggest tangible consequence for Lauren and Lee was "We're giving your truck, your pride and joy possession, to Buck." We stayed there for a moment, because we wanted them to feel the significance of that consequence.

GLENN: Why was this a consequence?

LAUREN: This was our truck! All of a sudden Buck, who did nothing to deserve the truck, gets our truck because we messed up!

GLENN: Did you feel this was unfair?

LAUREN: Yeah. Very. In my eyes, Buck didn't earn the truck. We messed up so bad that he got it from our faults. That came out of nowhere!

YVETTE: It stung!

LAUREN: Yeah. It hurt.

YVETTE: Then we swung it back around with "It's going to take some time for you to earn our trust back again. When we mess up, there's forgiveness and the need to restore trust and what that looks like. But we also want you to know what grace is about, and we bought a car for you guys." So Buck got the Ford Explorer, Lauren and Lee's pride and joy, and we bought the neighbor's Jetta so they could get to classes and get around.

LAUREN: Like, we're talking a dinosaur Jetta! (Laughter) Not like a new, cute, little Jetta. Nothing like that.

GLENN: Okay. How did you feel about this news?

LAUREN: It was like getting another shock. It was like, "Wait! We're getting a car?"

Lauren's Lessons

GLENN: Looking back, Lauren, these past five months since this happened, what is the one big thing you have learned from this experience?

LAUREN: There's a bunch of things. First, that I'm better than that. I know others do it, but I guess I have always prided myself on not doing it, and now I'm just as bad as them. This was disappointing to me. Till that time, I was able to say, "I've never been drunk. I haven't touched alcohol and stuff." Now I can't say that. I've also learned that I can have a lot of fun without alcohol and that I don't need it to have fun.

GLENN: What did you learn about Mom and Dad?

LAUREN: That no matter what I do, and how much I might mess up, I'll get their wrath, but they'll still be there for me. That I will be able to earn their trust back.

GLENN: Is there a wise word or something you would like to share with other parents? I mean, it's a tough job being a parent.

LAUREN: Right. Communication comes to mind.

YVETTE: Think of a situation with one of your friends who's struggling right now. If you could sit down with her parents, what would you like to be able to say?

LAUREN: Communication. Awareness. Don't be in denial of the fact that your kid would never do that or be capable of that.

Yvette's Lessons

GLENN: Okay, Yvette, your turn. If you were in a room with moms and dads right now, what would you want to say?

YVETTE: Make sure you're prepared to love them through the tough stuff, because it's inevitable. Tough stuff will also be in different forms. From drugs and alcohol, to eating disorders, to a broken heart from a boyfriend. But they abso-lutely have to know that they have a foundation that's rock-solid with you as their parent and that you're going to be there with them.

> Make sure you're prepared to love them through the tough stuff, because it's inevitable.

LAUREN: Right. Because if don't, they're going to find it otherwise, through alcohol and sleeping around and stuff. I know kids who turn to that because they don't have any support at home and no one to turn to.

YVETTE: Even if it costs you anxiety. You can't freak out. There have been times I have said to Tommy, "This is going to be a tough situation. We can freak out privately, but in front of our kids, we've got to hold it together. Our kids have to know that we're together in this and we're together *for* them and *with* them."

GLENN: I hear you saying that for parents it's critical that they're on the same page and consistent in the way they address issues with their children. You can't afford for one parent to parent a particular way and have the other parent in a totally different and contradictory way.

YVETTE: It was so important for Tommy and me to have that private time together before sitting down with our three children at the restaurant. We weren't so in sync that we knew how the other was going to intuitively respond in a pressured situation. We had to have a lot of drive time, private time to get on the same page.

GLENN: Final question. Looking back, do you think you could have done anything to better prepare Lauren and yourself to face something like this?

YVETTE: Honestly, I don't.

LAUREN: No, I would say they could have done nothing else. This was solely about my choice.

Conclusion

What a great testimony!

Yvette and Lauren gave us the inside scoop on their thoughts, motivations, emotions, and vulnerability as they went through Lauren's teenage years together. They also shared what lessons they took away from something that most of us as parents will never want to experience.

This story is real. And something like it happens every day for families everywhere. I hope you will be ready if it happens to you.

Chapter 10 Summary

Principles from Yvette and Lauren about letting children experience the consequences of poor decisions regarding drugs or alcohol:

- It's normal for parents to experience some uncertainty about how to deal with situations they've never encountered before involving drugs or alcohol.
- Spouses need to be intentional about getting on the same page before addressing the issue with their children.
- Parents shouldn't pretend that a negative situation with drugs or alcohol will resolve itself without their taking the time to work through it with their child.
- If parents remove the consequences, it will be at their child's expense.

- It's helpful to look for a moment, some time after the incident, to reflect on and reinforce some of the lessons learned.
- Parents need to extend grace to their children. This doesn't mean avoiding consequences. It means allowing the children to learn from what happened and to be given an opportunity to earn back the parents' trust.

CONCLUSION

Thanks for staying with me on this journey of discovery. You've seen for yourself how the best way for parents to protect their kids from the threats posed by drugs and alcohol is to maintain loving, informed two-way communication with them throughout their growing-up years. You should be feeling much more confident and competent now about having conversations with your kids that will help them make it into adulthood free of the harm that can come from these dangerous substances. And along the way, you've learned some principles that will serve you well when many other issues come up in parenting. I'm excited to think about your chances of walking through a safer, happier childhood with your young ones!

But you and I both know there are still challenges ahead as we try to help our children understand the choices that will keep them safe. Sometimes it can be lonely, confusing, and exhausting, while at other times it can be incredibly enriching. Whichever way it goes, our journey is far from over. And that is why I'm reminded of a word that came up in my interview with Yvette and Lauren: *grace*.

Giving grace is extending undeserved favor to a person who has let us down. It is an important practice to remember

Giving grace is an important practice to remember when our children disappoint us by experimenting with drugs or drink even after we have done our best to convince them not to.

when our children disappoint us by experimenting with drugs or drink even after we have done our best to convince them not to. As we have discussed in this book, they need to experience the consequences of their decisions if they are to learn from what happened. Yet, at the same time, they need loving acceptance from us. This kind of grace means our saying something like: "I'm going to forgive you in such a way that I'm going to forget that it happened and continue to show favor and blessing to you as my child. I have hope that you will grow from this experience and not let it negatively affect your future or our relationship."

Yet grace is not something that only our children need. We *all* need it on a regular basis.

Like Yvette and Lauren, I have seen the work of grace in my life. In fact, it is something I experience every day as a husband, father, colleague, and friend. On a personal level, it is waking up each morning knowing that God has blessed me with a new day and that his grace is available to me even though I don't deserve it. This is a miracle!

There are days when I know I don't deserve to be blessed with grace. I make lots of mistakes. I say things that are hurtful. Sometimes my actions are incredibly selfish, and I am relieved that nobody can read my thoughts, because I would be ashamed. I let my children down and at times do not show respect to my wife the way I should. I am prideful and some-times think I am more important than others. I worry about insignificant and worthless things, and I take every breath for granted. Get the picture? Maybe you can relate to what I'm saying.

My mother had a saying: "When there's nothing left, there's always room for a miracle." Perhaps you think you have failed as a parent and done a terrible job of raising your child. Maybe you think it's too late to turn things around, and no matter what you do, there is no way that your relationship with your child will be what you always dreamed it would be. *There's room for a miracle.*

In this book, I have talked about life not being an event but a journey. I pray that on your journey you will encounter a God who is more than you could ever hope for or imagine that he might be. Why? Because in the same way you extend grace to your child, God is willing to do the same for you. Jesus Christ, God's Son, took upon himself the consequences of your sin and self-centeredness that were preventing you from experiencing the life God wanted for you. It is as if God speaks to you those words of a parent to a child I just mentioned: "I'm going to forgive you in such a way that I'm going to forget that it happened and continue to show favor and blessing to you as my child. I have hope that you will grow from this experience and not let it negatively affect your future or our relationship."

That's real grace. Grace for the deepest needs within you. Grace for every area of your life.

To experience grace from a God who is not some im-personal object, distant Supreme Being, or cosmic controller, but rather a God who is real, also means there is no need to parent alone. The truth is, if you're like me, as you go about raising your children, you're going to need more wisdom, patience, strength, hope, and love than you have within yourself. Take heart in God's promise to never leave you alone on this journey nor withhold the resources you need. You just have to ask him!

> God promises to never leave you alone on this journey nor withhold the resources you need.

All this comes from the God who
settled the relationship between us and him,
and then called us to settle our
relationships with each other.
—2 Corinthians 5:18,
THE MESSAGE

"I know the plans I have for you,"
declares the LORD, "plans to prosper
you and not to harm you, plans to
give you hope and a future."
—Jeremiah 29:11,
NEW INTERNATIONAL VERSION

RESOURCES

Curriculum

How to Drug Proof Your Kids, a parenting curriculum by
Focus on the Family (www.drugproofyourkids.com)

Books

Biehl, Bobb, and Paul Swets. *Dreaming Big: Energizing
Yourself and Your Team with a Crystal-Clear Life
Dream.* Colorado Springs: Authentic, 2007.

Chapman, Gary. *The Five Love Languages of Teenagers.*
Chicago: Northfield, 2000.

Chapman, Gary, and Ross Campbell. *The Five Love
Languages of Children.* Chicago: Moody Press, 1997.

Chapman, Gary, with Derek Chapman. *Five Signs of a
Loving Family.* Chicago: Northfield, 1997.

Cloud, Henry, and John Townsend. *Boundaries Face to Face:
How to Have That Difficult Conversation You've Been
Avoiding.* Grand Rapids, MI: Zondervan, 2003.

———. *Boundaries with Kids: When to Say Yes, When to Say
No to Help Your Children Gain Control of Their Lives.*
Grand Rapids, MI: Zondervan, 1998.

———. *Boundaries with Teens: When to Say Yes, How to Say
No.* Grand Rapids, MI: Zondervan, 2006.

DeMoss, Mark. *The Little Red Book of Wisdom.* New York: MJF, 2009.

Dobson, James. *Preparing for Adolescence.* Ventura, CA: Gospel Light, 2006.

Hart, Archibald D. *Stress and Your Child.* Dallas: Word, 1992.

Lookadoo, Justin. *The Dirt on Drugs.* Grand Rapids, MI: Revell, 2005.

Parsons, Rob. *Helping Your Teenager Make It Through: What Every Parent Has to Know.* London: Hodder & Stoughton, 2009.

Reisser, Paul. *Complete Guide to Family Health, Nutrition & Fitness.* Carol Stream, IL: Tyndale, 2006.

Tobias, Cynthia Ulrich, and Carol Funk. *Bringing Out the Best in Your Child: 80 Ways to Focus on Every Kid's Strengths.* Ann Arbor, MI: Vine, 1997.

White, Joe, and Jim Weidmann, eds. *Parents' Guide to the Spiritual Mentoring of Teens.* Wheaton, IL: Tyndale, 2001.

Websites

How to Drug Proof Your Kids (www.drugproofyourkids.com)

Meth Project Foundation (www.methproject.org)

National Center on Addiction & Substance Abuse (www.casacolumbia.org)

National Institute on Drug Abuse (www.drugabuse.gov)

Partnership for a Drug Free America (www.drugfree.org, www.timetotalk.org)

Substance Abuse & Mental Health Services Administration (www.samhsa.gov)

Teen Challenge (www.teenchallengeusa.com)
Youth Service America (www.theantidrug.com)

NOTES

1. *Preventing Drug Use among Children and Adolescents*, 2nd ed., National Institute on Drug Abuse, October 2003, www.nida.nih. gov/prevention.

2. Raymond P. Daugherty and Carl Leukfeld, *Reducing the Risks for Substance Abuse: A Lifespan Approach* (New York: Plenum, 1998).

3. Arnold Lohaus, Marc Vierhaus, and Juliane Ball, "Parenting Styles and Health-Related Behavior in Childhood and Early Adolescence: Results of a Longitudinal Study," *Journal of Early Adolescence,* August 2009, 449.

4. The National Center on Addiction and Substance Abuse at Columbia University, "National Survey of American Attitudes on Substance Abuse XIV: Teens and Parents," August 2009, http:// www.casacolumbia.org/absolutenm/articlefiles/380-2009%20 Teen%20Survey%20Report.pdf. See also C. Jackson, L. Henriksen, D. Dickinson, and D. W. Levine, "The Early Use of Alcohol and Tobacco: Its Relation to Children's Competence and Parents' Behavior," Department of Health Behavior and Health Education, School of Public Health, University of North Carolina, 1997.

5. Yvette and Tommy chose to keep their daughter home rather than take her to the hospital. And it worked out all right for them. But if you are ever in a similar situation, and you think your child may be suffering from alcohol poisoning or a drug overdose, please consider the importance of getting medical care for your child. You

can always make sure your child has learned a lesson *after* getting his or her condition checked out by medical professionals.